Endorsements

A gift of words, and it is a gift beyond words. Join Paula in the pages as she walks each of us along a sacred path—through grief, yes, but more importantly, to the God whose endless grace paves each step.

—Tricia Lott Williford
Author, *And Life Comes Back*

Inspiring, encouraging and thought-provoking as Paula Freeman shares how she learned to live in "the unforced rhythms of grace" that her and our new lives as widows require.

—Gayle Roper
Author, *A Widow's Journey*
Founder, Widow's Weekend

Grief is messy and mysterious and pain-soaked; we want to run from its presence. But when after the loss of a lifelong love there's no place to run, the way ahead looks desperately lonely. In *Learning to Be Me Without You*, Paula Freeman offers gentle guidance and open-hearted companionship. Not by laying out a nine-step formula, but by sharing with naked vulnerability her own journey from brokenness into life as God's beloved.

—Maureen Rank
Author, *Free to Grieve: Healing and Encouragement for Those Who Have Suffered Miscarriage and Stillbirth*

Learning to Be Me Without You beautifully and powerfully describes the hard journey of widowhood. Paula is honest, thought-provoking, challenging, and gives permission to walk your grief journey on your own time schedule. You will be encouraged with a ray of hope and the promises of God, which will provide strength for your hurting heart.

—Sharon Engram and Lori Rohlinger
Authors, *Surviving Widowhood*

When our husband dies, our identity is shaken. In *Learning to Be Me Without You*, you will discover a friend who understands, a mentor offering wise counsel, and a gentle guide as Paula takes us by the hand through the valley of the shadow of death in the early days, months, and years of grief. You will be encouraged and challenged by the lessons Paula learned and is passing on from her transition from wife to widow.

—Lori Apon, Founder and Executive Director
Perspective Ministries and *WidowLife Magazines*

In *Learning To be Me Without You*, Paula Freeman pulls back the curtain of her life to show the deep pain and eventual heart transformation coming from the loss of her husband Ray. With honesty and humor, Paula's story reveals the conflicting messages within the church around loss and the unnecessary hurt that results. Paula brings her background as a social worker, nonprofit president, wife, and mom and cradles her experience in Scripture in a way that the reader finds understanding and hope as they walk their road of grief. I highly recommend this book to anyone looking for evidence of God at work in the hard seasons of life.

—Rev. Paul Lessard
Executive Minister, Evangelical Covenant Church

Our experience with loss may differ from the author's, but we can all probably admit that the transition to a "just me" life is full of challenges and sorrow. As Paula Freeman takes us on her widow's journey in *Learning to Be Me Without You*, she is honest about her struggles and the many unknowns she's faced. She shows us how God's grace trumped her fears, how she embraced God's "enough-ness" through surrender to Him, and how she recovered her life—in spiritual and practical ways. Her story offers hope and help for others on their own widows' journeys.

—Twila Belk, Writer and Speaker
Author, *Raindrops from Heaven* and *The Power to Be*

Learning to be Me Without You

Learning to be Me Without You

A Story of Love, Loss, and Coming Home

PAULA FREEMAN

REDEMPTION
PRESS

ISBN 13: 978-1-64645-807-3 (Paperback)
         978-1-64645-809-7
         978-1-64645-808-0

LCCN   2022907627

For my children:
Chad, Brooke, Nick, Tyler,
Hope, Sarah, and Abigail

In memory of Ray

We've all been made better
because he loved us.

Contents

Foreword: Tricia Lott Williford xi

Preface... xiii

Prologue... xvii

Part One: Tale of Two Islands

Chapter 1 Bora Bora 23

Chapter 2 Nobody I Need to Be 33

Chapter 3 Topsail.. 47

Chapter 4 Return to Topsail 57

Part Two: Setting Sail

Chapter 5 Passing Through 67

Chapter 6 Fishing.. 73

Chapter 7 Hours to Live 79

Chapter 8 Crisis of Faith 87

Chapter 9 Going Home 97

Chapter 10 Blessing of the Birds 105

Part Three: Into the Deep

Chapter 11 Solitude... 113

Chapter 12 Follow Me 121

Chapter 13 Rhythms of Grace 127

Chapter 14 Unsettled... 137

Chapter 15 Letting Go 145

Chapter 16 Beloved 155

Chapter 17 A New Kind of Broken................................ 163

Chapter 18 Song of the Ocean.. 171

Part Four: Safe Harbor

Chapter 19 Keeping It between the Ditches.................... 181

Chapter 20 Tending the Fire 189

Epilogue... 197

Acknowledgments 203

About the Author... 207

Endnotes.. 209

Foreword

For a long time, *widow* was a hard word for me to say. Not because it's a difficult word to pronounce, of course, but because I didn't want the word to be mine.

I lost my husband when I was thirty-one years old and he was thirty-five. The doctors thought he had the flu, and they sent us home from the hospital with the promise, "He won't die from this, but he'll feel like it." They were only partly right. The flu had masked the symptoms of an infection in his bloodstream, and he died the next morning, on our bedroom floor.

He was sick for just twelve hours from beginning to end; it all happened so fast.

He was gone before the paramedics could get there.

Our little boys were five and three, not yet in kindergarten.

It was two days before Christmas.

He was so suddenly gone.

And a new word entered my regular vocabulary: *widow*.

I lovingly refer to the Widows Club as the Worst Club Ever. Nobody wants to be in it. But let me tell you: the sisterhood inside this community is a tapestry of strong, fierce women who are doing the hard work of grieving well.

Because it is hard work. It really, truly is.

Not everyone understands grief. The people who don't understand—well, they give you a little time, yes. They have their measure of grace for you in that first year, when they expect you to need a little space, a little time, a few meals in the freezer. But after that, they want you to push through. They want you to bounce back, even if your rubber band has lost elasticity. They want you to flip the lights back on and get on with your life. The grace people give one another often has an expiration date, even in grief.

But the grace of God—thicker than even the deepest sadness—is a blanket we can rest in. He meets us in the journey, and he doesn't rush us through. He is patient, kind, and present. After all, Psalm 68:5 reminds us that he is a "father to the fatherless, a defender of widows—this is God." So the members of the Worst Club Ever have a special place in his heart.

Grief doesn't go away because you ignore it. And neither does God. What a precious truth that is.

Paula's story is a gift of words, and it is a gift *beyond* words. Join her in the pages, as she walks each of us along a sacred path: through grief, yes, but most importantly, to the God whose endless grace paves each step.

—Tricia Lott Williford, author of *And Life Comes Back*

Preface

In all their suffering,
He suffered, and the Angel
of His Presence saved them.
Isaiah 63:9 HCSB

My husband Ray and I moved from the Colorado foothills to coastal North Carolina eighteen months after he was diagnosed with interstitial lung disease. He could breathe better at sea level. Even his pulmonologist agreed that Colorado was a great place to live but a lousy place to breathe. We decided to make this our last big adventure and headed for the beach.

Ray died two weeks after we moved. His sudden homegoing left me alone, halfway across the country from family and friends. A house full of boxes to unpack, a funeral to plan, the administration of dying to tackle, our Colorado home to sell, and the unenviable task of grieving my husband's death upended life as I had known it.

I journaled to help process these changes. I recorded events and emotions I might otherwise forget. Writing led me to discover truths about myself and find God in my story. Writing helped me heal. Eventually, I shared snippets with others who encouraged me to keep writing. And I did.

I wrote this book for widows and others who may one day lose their spouse; for those who have experienced grief and loss, whatever the source; and for anyone who desires a deeper, more authentic relationship with Jesus based on transformation, not information. I have written a book I wish I could have read.

Learning to Be Me Without You chronicles my spiritual journey during the nineteen months I lived in North Carolina after Ray's death and wrestled with these questions: How can I survive this loss? Will God be enough? And why am I here? This is a story about God's extraordinary faithfulness to one ordinary widow: a faithfulness tailor-made for my surviving heart. It's about finding the presence of God in the wilderness of widowhood and the life-changing difference it can make.

Some seven hundred thousand American women lose their spouses each year.[1] When Ray died, I involuntarily joined ranks with an estimated 13.6 million widows in the United States.[2] These numbers will only rise as baby boomers age and die. *Learning to Be Me Without You* is a candid account of the impact one death makes and offers hope for others who mourn—an antidote to our culture that does not deal well with death or grieving.

I faced two problems in telling this story. The first was how to convey the chaos, drama, and warts of real life and marriage alongside the best life has to offer. What do I include, and what do I leave out?

After Ray died, I had to take an honest look at myself before I could go forward. To reconcile regret, I had to own the ways I had hurt him and others. Ray had been an imperfect man, husband, and father who described himself as "a knight in somewhat tarnished armor." We had our share of disagreements over our forty-two-year marriage, and we said and did things that deeply hurt each other. We differed on how to manage money and how to spend a Saturday. Ray lived in the present and took a "good enough" approach to most things; I was the future-oriented perfectionist. He withdrew when stressed, while I cussed and pedaled faster. At one point, we worked with a counselor to learn how to manage conflict in healthy ways. Ray and I loved and sometimes disagreed passionately. Occasionally it got messy.

I do not want to deify or dishonor Ray. I do want to show what my family and I lost when he died. But more importantly, I long to tell the story of how God met me in my deepest sorrow and how he recovered my life from loss.

The second problem I faced was finding the language to describe the mystery of how God did that. Each faith tradition has its own pool of words and phrases to describe this mystery. Yet I frequently found words inadequate. Those I ultimately chose might not be the best ones, or even the most accurate, but my attempt to choose well was both honest and arduous.

My daily prayer in writing this memoir has been *Lord, help me show the essence of how you worked in my life, so others might see You in theirs.*

Thank you for picking up this book. I pray that my story might become a vehicle that graciously carries you into your own. May you find not only language for your sorrows, but God's presence within them. You are deeply loved and cherished. If you hear God's whispered invitation to go on a further journey with him, I pray you say "Yes."

If there is anything here to ease your journey, praise God. For that which causes angst, I ask your forgiveness. Whoever you are, and wherever you find yourself, know that I have been praying for you. I wrote this story with you in mind. Read it with your heart, as a gift. Read it alone, as a couple, or in a small group. Spend time with the Quiet Reflection questions at the end of each chapter. And be encouraged.

With much love,

Paula

Prologue

His loved ones are very precious to him,
and he does not lightly let them die.
Psalm 116:15 TLB

September 12, 2015
Duke Medical Center, Durham, North Carolina

"Mom, I think you need to come—now!"

Tyler, one of my sons, towered over me and gently touched my shoulder. "Dad . . ." He turned toward the hospital bed in the center of the small ICU room—my husband's bed that I had kept vigil beside through the night.

I had held and studied his hands through the lifeless metal rails as I tried to grasp and prolong the moments with him. Those hands perfectly fit mine. They had loved and comforted me, cradled our babies, carved Thanksgiving turkeys, taught our sons to fish, and patiently combed knots out of our daughters' long, tangled hair.

Now, before the sun set on this day, they would be gone.

My greatest fear was coming to pass. *Ray is going to die and leave me alone. I don't think I can survive this loss!*

When my cell phone rang and I heard our pastor's voice calling from Colorado, I stepped aside to the lone window framing the surreal normalcy of other people's lives several stories below.

"He's not going to make it," I told him when he asked about Ray. "He'll probably die today."

In the time it took to say those words, something changed. I clutched the tear-soaked blanket draping my shoulders and rushed to Ray's bedside. He was slumped, unconscious, but I knew. I wanted to crawl through the railing, untangle wires and tubes, and soak him in. *How close can I get?* I leaned into him and caressed his face and head, breathing in the smell of him.

"I'm walking you home, baby. I'm walking you home," I whispered into his ear, feeling life leave. "I think he's gone," I sobbed to my sons sharing this holy ground.

My son Nick rose, seeking confirmation from the "dying team" who watched outside our door, monitoring everything living and dying in Ray's body.

"No, not quite," one said. "Almost."

How do you do this dying thing? There are no do-overs. *Lord, help me. Help me do this letting go well.*

Uninvited and barely noticed, a doctor draped in a white coat stepped into his room. Rubber soles carried her silently to his bedside—our bedside. Sensing her presence and the fading of his, I looked up into unfamiliar eyes that were neither kind nor harsh—a trespasser for a time in our story.

"May I examine his eyes?"

I nodded, returning my gaze to Ray's face, continuing to caress it, willing my hands and eyes to remember the feel of it: its warmth, blended textures of graying cheek stubble and life-etched creases, crow's-feet that crinkled when he smiled, salt-and-pepper full goatee trimmed close, one he longed to grow years before I agreed. I continued to pour love into his ears, hoping he could hear—or see with resurrection eyes.

"The time of death is 9:48," noted the doctor. Ray had peacefully left his tent.

We sat, my sons and I, silent, surrendering in our own ways to this overwhelming grief.

"I want to pray," I finally said, reaching for the man-hands of our once-little boys. I needed to give thanks in the face of death, to stake my claim on the hope of our grand reunion at the end of this long goodbye.

Tears blanketed the sheet at the foot of his bed as we bowed our heads. "Thank you, Father, for Ray's life, for your gift of him to me, and to our family. Have mercy on us and help us learn to do life without him. May your presence become greater than his absence."

Then we left, walking wordlessly through sterile hallways that delivered us into a waiting room filled with family members and strangers who hoped our story would not become theirs.

9:48.

After forty-two years, three months, and ten days of marriage, I must remember when it stopped—the clock of life as I'd known it.

But the countdown had begun years before.

Part One

Tale of Two Islands

*Come with me by yourselves
to a quiet place and get some rest.*
Mark 6:31b

*Have I not commanded you?
Be strong and courageous.
Do not be afraid;
do not be discouraged,
for the LORD your God will
be with you wherever you go.*
Joshua 1:9

Bora Bora

Your path led through the sea,
your way through the mighty waters,
though your footprints were not seen.
Psalm 77:19

June 1998

Our happy place was the beach. Any beach. We had discovered its magic, the transforming power of surf and sand, on business trips and family vacations.

Ray and I needed that magic when we arrived in the small, romantic South Pacific island paradise of Bora Bora to celebrate our twenty-fifth wedding anniversary. We savored the thought of long, hand-in-hand beach walks, lingering breakfast talks, Tahiti punch before noon, and just enough snorkeling and bicycle riding to convince our bodies we'd exercised.

Unpacking our suitcases would be easy. But the baggage we brought might take longer. Exhausted from our two-career marriage and a large family that had been recently hijacked by teenage hormones and adoption realities, we craved rest, relief, and romance.

We met Hans on our second day in paradise. He was our neighbor, renting the beachside bungalow next to ours. A quiet man of average build, he sported neatly cropped hair above dark eyebrows. Reflective and observant, his understated elegance and confidence bespoke a man comfortable in his own skin yet accustomed to the respect and deference of others.

But he was alone. Alone in paradise. This unsettled me.

I don't remember when Hans shared his story with us, only that it made me sad. Not just a little sad, but a sadness that welled up, sank deep, and clung hard. A retired attorney from Sweden, Hans and his wife of fifty-seven years had planned to take this trip together, he explained. But she had died two months earlier. So he came alone.

Sorrow choked me. *Good for you*, I thought. *How brave.*

Then I watched, helpless, as grief invaded the space reserved for anniversary memories. I couldn't let it go or escape its grip on me. The anguish of Hans's story reeled me in through undefinable ways. Was it the same morbid curiosity that made me slow down and rubberneck a roadside accident? Or perhaps it was like being glued to television news as horrific images splash across the screen when I really want to cover my eyes, plug my ears, and babble nonsense to protect my heart from feelings that threaten to collide with my deepest fears.

Hans's story—no, the sorrow of his aloneness—rattled me long and hard. And I began to own Hans's pain. *What made him come alone?* I wondered as I stood on the beach later that day, watching him bob in the turquoise ocean outside our bungalows, a minuscule piece of life's ebb and flow—collateral damage trapped in his own life.

The grief of his amputated life, and implications for my future, blindsided me later that week when Ray and I strolled to a nearby restaurant for dinner. Stepping from the balmy night air into the intimate, dimly lit lobby, we saw Hans at a table set for one. We smiled and exchanged greetings with him as I clutched Ray's hand, then followed the hostess to our table. Once we were seated, the claustrophobic urge to scratch and fight against an encroaching threat consumed me. *No! Not my life! Not my man!* And I sensed an unavoidable truth lay itself down beside my happily-ever-after life. An in-your-face, solid reality that stole my breath as I choked back stinging tears: death would separate Ray and me too. But I didn't want to think about that. Not then. Not ever.

That was when I first acknowledged the internal tensions of parallel tracks—opposites that coexist in our lives and race side by side through time and conflicting realities: blessing and adversity, joy and sorrow, success and failure, life and death.

I loved living within the mystery of marriage—its physical, soulful belonging; the blending, compromising, growing-better-together-than-we-can-be-alone manifestation of our created-ness. But sadness began to walk in sync with beach magic that night—parallel tracks engraving themselves into the fabric of my soul.

Hans personified my deepest fear, the one I had spent twenty-five years trying to ignore. The one I didn't think I could survive.

Summer 1971

I found my summer job in the back of the high school biology room with the student teacher.

As a lab assistant for Mr. Cookson, a short, gray-haired, no-nonsense teacher who was well liked, deeply respected, and nearing retirement, my responsibilities included grading papers with his student teacher, a man who had been a ranger in Rocky Mountain National Park.

I was a Kansas girl. But my love affair with Colorado began the summer I attended a family camp at the YMCA of the Rockies in Estes Park with my parents when I was five. It's where

I learned to sing "John Jacob Jingleheimer Schmidt" while gazing into a campfire as lazy sparks rebelled, popped, then sputtered into nothingness. A memory sopping with warmth and belonging.

I returned to Colorado with family and friends throughout my growing-up years, mainly to ski. I came to faith in Christ at a Young Life spring-break ski camp my junior year in high school. I even planned to attend college in Colorado with my best friend, Carol, after she and I made a road trip to visit several schools. She wanted to be a doctor; I wanted to leave Kansas.

As the ex-forest ranger and I graded papers during that final semester of my senior year, we talked about Colorado. I listened to his adventures and told him I hoped to work there too. He offered names and phone numbers of people to contact. And I did. Shortly after graduation, my parents drove me to Grand Lake, Colorado, where I spent the summer with more than one hundred college students from all over the United States, as part of the Grand Lake Lodge summer crew.

Some worked at the lodge as waiters or housekeepers or on the maintenance team; others, like me, greeted tourists and sold souvenirs at the Alpine Visitor Center atop Trail Ridge Road in Rocky Mountain National Park. It didn't matter where we clocked in. We all had flocked to Colorado for the experience of a lifetime.

Despite chilling mountain temperatures and being able to see our breath on summer mornings, female staff was required to wear a company-issued denim lederhosen—hot pants of respectable length—a white top, and a red, white, and blue scarf.

Each morning, various body shapes and sizes, clad in identical uniforms hidden beneath winter coats, gripped Styrofoam cups of steaming coffee to thaw cold hands. Reluctantly, we abandoned the warmth of the staff dining room to squeeze into waiting station wagons that, forty-five minutes later, would deliver us to the visitor's center nearly twelve thousand feet above sea level. Every evening, these same cars, driven by male crew members, drove us "home." We passed through tundra, woodlands, and past animal watering holes as we wound through mountains and meadows, then out of Rocky Mountain National Park onto the lane that led to the lodge.

I made little money but many friends that summer. I lived in "The Penthouse," a dilapidated barn that had been converted into a rustic dormitory for female employees. My job, which included meeting and visiting with tourists from the United States and abroad, was pure fun. During days off I explored the local area, rode horseback on forest trails and across broad meadows, hiked mountains in the park, and attended concerts and Coors tours in Denver. It was a coming-of-age summer that tested my values and provided countless opportunities to live them: wilderness camp, perpetual frat party, freshman year in college with free love tumbling over from the sixties crammed into ninety days of an outrageously fun time.

Then it was over.

I flew home, binge-washed laundry, repacked, and left for college the next day. I had decided to follow a young man to the University of Arkansas instead of my best friend to Colorado.

For the second time in three months, I was on my own in a new place.

Julie, a sophomore, was one of the first people I met when I arrived. She lived two doors down from me in the dorm. "A few friends and I are going to church this evening," she said, peeking around the doorway into my room as I continued to unpack. "Would you like to come?"

"Sure," I said. I was interested in spiritual things since my coming-to-faith experience in Colorado, and I wanted to meet new people.

As Julie and I pushed through the front doors of our dorm

later that evening and stepped into the courtyard that separated it from the narrow, two-lane, car-lined street in front, I saw a guy sauntering toward us. I noted his full, dark beard, receding hairline, casual swagger, faded jeans, and the smile that reached his eyes with a hint of mischief. He was Julie's friend who would take us to church that night.

Ray was a senior, a student leader with Campus Crusade for Christ, now called Cru. He told me years later that what he remembered of our first meeting was my broad and muscular shoulders from eight years of competitive swimming. Other than that, he was just a ride to church.

Winter 1972

Laughter filled my college dorm room one dateless Friday night when several girls spontaneously gathered to commiserate on our shared fate. Lively banter erupted as each tried to outdo the others in naming the most outrageous contenders for what-if fantasy dates: those dates most likely to never happen.

Sitting atop my built-in desk, legs dangling over the side and facing the others, I tossed them my contribution. "Who knows?" I said. "I might even date Ray Freeman!"

The thought had never occurred to me before that moment. Although by then Ray and I were participating in many of the same Christian student activities, ours was a casual friendship. He was an acquaintance, a senior—not in my orbit. And I was not inclined to question the order of the universe. Sharing silliness and laughter among friends that night, his was the most unlikely name I could think of to make my fantasy-date point. Absurd. A throw-away comment.

Several days later, two friends from that Friday-night gathering poked their heads into my room. "Hey, we're planning to go home for the weekend," one said. "Wanna come?"

"I'd love to, but not this weekend," I replied. "I have a date on Saturday night." With the young man I had followed to college.

Shortly after they left on Friday, however, the order of the universe shifted. Ray called. "Would you like to go to the Nitty Gritty Dirt Band concert on campus tonight?"

"Sure," I said. It was late notice, but it beat spending another Friday night in the dorm. It wasn't a date, just something to do with a friend.

We sat through the concert on backless bleachers in the field-house rafters, then drove to the basement apartment he shared with a roommate. Two Cru friends shared the upper floor of the dumpy, off-campus house struggling to survive a string of college-boy tenants. We drank coffee and visited into the wee hours of the morning. I would be in trouble!

College dormitories enforced strict curfews in the seventies—especially girls' dorms in the south. After my "Rocky Mountain high" summer in Colorado, I thought I'd outgrown such nonsense. Curfews were ridiculous—until they weren't. I learned how irrelevant my opinion was when I stood before the dormitory disciplinary board later that week.

But as Ray drove me back to the dorm in those early-morning hours, we made plans to go hiking later that day. He picked me up midmorning on Saturday (it was a date!) knowing I had to be back in time for my date with the young man I had followed to college.

My friends returned on Sunday, forty-eight hours after they had left. "Boy, do I have a story for you!" I said when they stopped by my room. I *was* dating Ray Freeman.

Ray and I became inseparable as friendship blossomed into romance. We discussed marriage and looked at rings before the end of the school year, but we pursued our respective summer plans after his May graduation.

Ray drove with friends to Southern California to attend staff training with Cru. Back home in Kansas, I lifeguarded, taught swim lessons, and helped lead a junior-high youth group. Daily letters and pay-by-the-minute phone calls strengthened our relationship and deepened our longing to be together. I couldn't wait to see him.

As summer break was winding down, I watched a full August moon lift itself above the horizon and dominate the darkening sky outside my bedroom window. I would soon return to college. But that night, as I gazed at the moon shining over Ray as he sped from California to Kansas, I knew. It wasn't an idea to ponder or a decision to make, but a whole, fully formed *knowing* in the center of my soul: Ray would ask me to marry him. And I would say yes.

Things veered wildly off course, however, a few days after he arrived.

"I listened to the radio as I drove through the night to get here," he mentioned as we strolled, hand in hand, through a city park the day before he planned to leave. "And it seemed like every other song was about breaking up. I began to wonder if that was what God was trying to tell us. That we should break up. What do you think?" he asked, turning to me as we walked while continuing to hold hands. Ray had asked that question as if he might be wondering whether I wanted cream or sugar in my coffee, oblivious to the grenade he'd lobbed.

I don't remember how I responded. He once chuckled and said I "didn't take it very well." I never thought to ask more, given how things turned out.

Minutes before saying goodbye the next morning, stalling for time before this next goodbye, Ray and I meandered to the hill overlooking the lake and woods behind my family home. A sweltering sun had baked the ground on which we walked, and the heat and humidity were already stifling. Steeped in thought, we stopped and leaned against Dad's tractor parked outside the backyard fence. Breaking our comfortable silence, Ray turned to me and said, "Will you marry me?"

"Are you serious?" I asked, recalling yesterday's doubts.

He was.

"Then yes," I said, like I knew I would.

While not the most romantic proposal, it did rank high in uniqueness. It was also the most natural, inevitable unfolding of our relationship, one breath following another. I couldn't imagine my life without him. It suited us.

After a ten-month, long-distance engagement, Ray and I married in June 1973. We were eager to begin our married life on a campus ministry team at the University of Iowa, where I would also be a full-time student.

Somewhere between "Then yes" and "I do," the fear that Ray would die and leave me alone took root. I never spoke of it and resisted thinking about it. On those occasions when I reluctantly acknowledged its presence, I knew a deeper fear lurked within its shadows: I didn't think I could survive the grief of his death if he did.

Maybe, if I tried hard, prayed right, and did enough good things, God would pass over my house when he doled out sorrow and suffering. I thought it was worth a try. So I tried really, really hard—for twenty-five years.

Then Hans. Alone in paradise. Alone in turquoise water. Alone in candlelight at a table set for one on a trip planned for two.

It wasn't Hans's grief I bore on Bora Bora. It was the beginning of my own.

Quiet Reflections

- What is one fear in your life you haven't wanted to face? When did it begin?

- What do you believe will happen if you name and acknowledge this fear? Where did that thought or belief come from?

- What has been your strategy to avoid suffering? How has it helped or hindered your relationship with God?

Nobody I Need to Be

He has watched over your journey
through this vast wilderness.
These forty years the LORD your God has been with
you, and you have not lacked anything.
Deuteronomy 2:7

January 2014, Colorado

"So, where do you want to go for your retirement vacation?"
Ray asked one Saturday morning as I walked into the room.
He peered over the top of his computer and took another sip of
coffee as he waited for my response.

"I want to rent a house on the beach in North Carolina," I
said, my answer whole and complete, unhesitating, as if I'd rehearsed it countless times.

I'd been infatuated with islands ever since reading *Misty of
Chincoteague* by Marguerite Henry as a ten-year-old who loved
horses. Although I later learned Chincoteague was part of Virginia, I still wanted to go to North Carolina.

"For a month," I added. "And let's take Annie and make it a road trip."

Ray and I had agreed, "No more dogs!" when our two standard poodles died the previous year within days of each other on the brink of our empty nest. "Or anything else that depends on me to feed it," I added. After more than thirty-eight years of parenting seven children and raising countless pets, our empty-nest finish-line taunted me, dangling its handsome carrot before my eyes. I was ready to sprint unencumbered to claim my prize—this man all to myself.

Ray and I had raised our family on five wooded acres south-west of Denver—a pet magnet. We had sheltered our share of them: dogs, including two who birthed puppies; a cat who de-livered four kittens on the foot of our youngest son's bed as he slept; a guinea pig named Cleveland; two hamsters the pet store owner assured us were female but who nevertheless, bred and had babies; a plethora of fish; two bunnies, Lucy and Blossom; four ducks, whose untimely deaths traumatized our kids; and Thomas, the aquatic turtle that made me scream the morning he inexplica-bly turned up in my shower.

Ray and I said yes to pet requests as often as we could, with one caveat clearly understood between the two of us: said pet's life expectancy could not exceed our last child leaving home. With six children launched and the youngest in college, our looming empty nest implied . . . well, empty.

No. More. Dogs.

Until Annie.

The dog we said we'd never get. The one we promised would not come as a surprise from one of us to the other. The one who had wiggled her soft, cuddly self into our hearts a few months earlier and forced us to reconsider the no-pet, empty-nest policy.

Ray was the culprit.

"Who's that?" I asked several months earlier when he handed me his iPad, the screen filled with a picture of a smiling, dark-haired little boy clutching a fluffy ball of fur.

"It's your new puppy," he said. "An apricot standard poodle."

"No, I mean who's *this*?" I persisted, pointing to the boy, oblivious to the dog.

"It's your new puppy," Ray insisted, smiling sheepishly.

Although we had promised each other no such surprises, that was before Ray thought I needed her. My father was dying. Extended family drama engulfed us, threatening to deplete our emotional bank accounts. A puppy to love might be a healthy deposit to offset the taxing withdrawals.

"And," Ray added, weighing the consequences of his infraction, "I've only paid a deposit for her, so you can always say no. By the way, that cute little boy? He's the breeder's son."

Well then. Maybe it wasn't a broken promise but a bent one, equipped with an escape clause to fit a new set of circumstances. I loved him for taking that risk and didn't say no.

Six months later, on that Saturday morning in January, as we planned my retirement vacation, only one obstacle remained: I needed to retire. No one was taking bets on how well I would do that. Or if I even could.

For as long as I can remember, I wanted to adopt children from different countries and races. I've never understood why. But over the years I've come to believe God placed that dream in my heart so he could be the one to fulfill it.

That dream lay dormant as Ray and I dated, married, and began our family. First a son, then a daughter, and two more sons. Ray transitioned from working in Christian ministry to outside sales in the clothing business. I was a full-time mom, our lives rich and full.

Yet nestled within that fertile ground of contentment, almost unnoticed, my adoption dream began to stir. It flirted with the fringes of my imagination and then exploded into desire as Ray settled into naively believing our family was complete. Until he didn't.

"Have you been praying for me?" he asked one afternoon, out of the blue, as we waited in line at a drive-through bank window.

Surprised, I hesitated. How do you answer a question like that? *"No, honey, I'm sorry. I haven't."* Or *"Of course I have!"* I settled on "Yes, but why do you ask?"

"Because I'm ready to be a giver," he said.

We both knew that meant adoption. Stutter steps and false starts littered our way until we read an announcement in our church bulletin from an adoption agency seeking families for six little girls in India.

Boom!

We jumped through countless hoops. Prayed. Waited. Until finally, in September 1987, we flew to India to meet our nine-month-old daughter, Hope, and bring her home—never giving a thought to the impact her adoption, and India, might have on us.

Our plane taxied and came to rest at a seemingly arbitrary spot on the runway when we landed in Hyderabad, a major city in south-central India. Swallowed up by scorching heat as we descended steep metal stairs to the tarmac below, my clothes felt as if they were melting and hung heavily on my body. We passed armed soldiers standing at attention, guns stretching skyward above their heads as we trudged to the terminal. There we inched our way in serpentine lines to clear immigration and customs, then entered the brawl of baggage claim before emerging from the airport into a pulsing mass of humanity.

Desperation engulfed us. Beggars in tattered rags swarmed the parking lot and nearby sidewalks. Starving mothers with sunken cheeks and pleading eyes cradled emaciated children in one arm, the other outstretched—palms up. Relentless noise, the clamoring, pushing, shoving, and yelling from those wanting to help us with our luggage for a rupee's tip assaulted our senses.

The following day, Ray and I, along with a diminutive elderly Indian nun, sat in the back seat of an aging taxi as it crawled through horn-blaring traffic. Finally, after forever, it sputtered to a stop in front of a neglected, low-slung, concrete building made invisible by towering hedges and its inhabitants, whom society refused to see. Orphans.

The nun, who would become Grandma Vasantha to our family, had cared for Hope when she arrived as a newborn, near death, at a Christian foundling home in Hyderabad. This saint would later wrap one arm around me, shake her other fist defiantly, and exclaim in her thick accent, "For three months, day and night, I prayed God would save this baby!" But that day, she was taking us to meet our daughter.

Anticipation nearly suffocated me as I stepped from the car. Yet despite our excitement, no one spoke. This was it. Almost. Only one rickety screen door separated Ray and me from our daughter and the moment about which I had dreamed. A prolonged squeaking of rusty door hinges announced our arrival as Grandma Vasantha pulled it open and we crossed a battered threshold into the government orphanage.

Rows of small metal cribs with chipped paint filled the singular room. Too many children and not enough adults to care for them. I stood, searching, trying to match the image of the small face in the black-and-white photo that hung on our refrigerator back home with one of these precious children. Then I saw her.

My arms developed a mind of their own and scooped her up. Cradled her. I inhaled the scent of her and kissed her soft, brown cheeks.

During our two-week stay in India, we held more beautiful children orphaned for unimaginable reasons: mothers who died from childbirth, a cobra bite, poverty or disease, and cultural taboos against single parenting.

I knew then, as surely as I had known that August night in Kansas—with a whole, fully formed knowing in the center of my soul that Ray would ask me to marry him and I would say yes—that every child deserves a family regardless of the country or circumstances into which they were born.

Ray and I had come to India to get our daughter, return home to four waiting children, and live happily ever after. So focused were we on living out this script that we never saw it coming—the adjustment, change, unexpected challenges, and new direction our lives would take.

Invisible children opened our eyes. We had seen the heart of God.

Life gobbled us up when we got home. Identifying and meeting the needs of a new baby who was developmentally delayed because of institutional deprivation created a parallel track to the existing rhythms of our young family. There was school, after-school sports, work and homework, carpools, meals, and laundry. Oh, the laundry for a family of seven.

The crisis of the immediate, and accommodating our respective bandwidths for stress and chaos, allowed Ray and me to temporarily ignore two significant questions: What would be our response to what we had seen in India? And what would I do as an encore to parenting when mothering years were over? The answers to both occurred organically.

Although Hope did come home, our adoption process left much to be desired. The last straw came in a phone call from our agency. They wanted more money despite the terms of the service contract we had signed.

This isn't right! I silently screamed as the director droned on, carefully crafting her justification for breaking a contract. *I'm going to start an adoption agency,* I vowed. *Other adoptive parents shouldn't have to go through what we did.* It was a knee-jerk reaction to anger and frustration.

Something took root, however, in the thinking of it, and I sat on this idea like a broody hen. Waiting. Wondering. Imagining what this might mean for me and our family. Between carpool runs, checking homework, and packing lunches, I prayed and researched state licensing requirements for adoption agencies and how to start a nonprofit organization.

One Saturday morning, several months after returning home from India, Ray and I went to breakfast to unpack this idea of me applying to graduate school to earn my master of social work degree, one of the countless requirements to license an adoption agency in Colorado. Although neither of us could anticipate its full impact on our marriage and family, by the time the waitress returned with our bill, Ray reached for my hands across the table, looked squarely into my eyes, and said, "Sweetheart, you have my blessing."

One year later, in the fall of 1988, I started graduate school, one decade and five children after I had last crossed the threshold of a college classroom. Two years later, in 1990, Hope's Promise, a licensed adoption agency and orphan care ministry, hatched.

From the outset Ray served on its board of directors. Sometimes, during my tenure as its executive director, when I traveled to develop international programs, recruit and train indigenous staff members, and launch our adoption and orphan care ministries, he went with me. But most of the time, in addition to his own demanding career, he managed the zoo—kids and pets back home—and prayed for my safe and speedy return.

Through the years, our children volunteered for Hope's Promise, flipped hamburgers at agency picnics, donated from their allowances, and shared their bedrooms when we hosted international staff members. Our oldest daughter, Brooke, graduated from college with her social work degree and became a caseworker. Hope's Promise wove itself into the fabric of our family rhythms and identity, and it grew.

Our family did too, when, in the mid-nineties, we adopted two more daughters: Sarah, a three-year-old from Cambodia, and Abigail, a sixteen-month-old from India. That was when Hope's Promise became the eighth child in our family.

So as Ray and I planned our trip to the North Carolina coast on that Saturday morning in January, taking the prerequisite step to retire was no small thing. It would suck a hole out of me big enough to drive a truck through. Could a month at the beach begin to fill it?

I recalled the opening words of my letter of resignation to our board of directors as my final day with Hope's Promise drew near:

> It has been my privilege and honor to serve this organization as its founder and executive director for over 23 years. It has truly been a labor of love for me and my family. Therefore, with mixed emotions, and the Lord's peace, I respectfully submit my letter of resignation as executive director.

It sounded good. But it wasn't all true.

I did love our mission, my work, and the people with whom I served; they had become a second family. But it hadn't always been a labor of love. Sometimes it was hard and conflicted, held together by worn-out threads of a lifelong mantra: *quitters never win, and winners never quit.* Sometimes I wanted to run far, far away.

Seduced by a lie of my generation, I had convinced myself its whispers might be true. Maybe I *could* have it all: marriage, family, and career. Although motivated and organized, hardwired to set goals and think strategically, I grossly underestimated the relentless demands of starting an organization and overestimated my limited ability to deliver.

I also remained clueless about emotional wounds that lurked beneath the surface. I felt exhausted, overwhelmed, beat up, and angry. Life wasn't supposed to be this hard, especially when you tried to do something good.

Ray and I had moseyed into adoptive parenthood with many of the same expectations we held for our biological children: we would love them and be loved in return; healthy children would blossom in our loving, Christian family; seasoned parenting skills would prove sufficient for the task; and our marriage would thrive. We were wrong on all counts.

One of our daughters suffered from a mental illness that compromised her ability to attach to other people in emotionally healthy ways. Trauma she sustained in her early years and the deprivation she experienced at the orphanage contributed to her challenges. The resulting drama and chaos wreaked havoc in our home for years and affected every member of our family. The stress it created gnawed holes in our marriage; I also resented the inequitable distribution of my parenting time and energy, and so did others. Teenage sons judged Ray and me for how we parented their younger sisters, and they tested behavioral boundaries. Sometimes our daughter harmed herself and others. And I was her target. I wrote about this as an adoption social worker in *A Place I Didn't Belong: Hope for Adoptive Moms.*

> Once the bond between a child and biological mother is broken, some children determine to protect themselves from further trauma at all costs. Deep in their soul they resolve not to have another mom (they still need a maid, cook, and chauffeur; they just won't allow emotional intimacy or control.) Mom then becomes the target of her child's rejection because she represents the greatest threat to the child's defenses . . . While they [adopted children] fear abandonment, they may also test it with a vengeance. If they can get mom to reject them, it validates their primal fear of being defective, and that they will be rejected and abandoned.[3]

This prolonged rejection from my daughter fueled a fear of failure that had taken root early in my life. So I had tried harder, prayed louder, and generally wore myself out. Adoption hadn't turned out the way I thought it would as unmet expectations collided with realities. Fear for my daughter's future and the health of my family consumed me. I felt inadequate and ashamed for not being a "good enough" mother.

I ran myself ragged for nearly a decade until I found myself, as Parker Palmer describes in *Let Your Life Speak*, in "the dark woods called clinical depression, a total eclipse of light and hope . . . the ultimate state of disconnection."[4] Isolated. Alone. Broken.

Yet into that brokenness seeped life-changing grace. It started with a question.

Ray's concern for my well-being, coupled with knowing I was in trouble, led me to professional counseling. After several weeks of meeting with Carol, I responded to one of her probing questions as truthfully as I knew how. It wasn't pretty.

"But Paula," she gently persisted, "where's the grace?"

"I have no idea," I said, scraping the bucket of painful confession. "It's not a part of my experience." But in the saying, I knew something was missing, something really important that I needed.

The next morning, I poured a cup of coffee and walked downstairs to my home office. Closing the door behind me, I pulled a concordance from the bookshelf, settled into my reading chair, and looked up the word *grace*. Beginning at the top of the list of all the Bible verses on grace, I began to write them out in my journal, one verse after another. I soaked in the consistent, life-giving message—living water on parched desert sand—for my unquenchable thirst. I prayed, *Father, help me receive your grace. And help me learn to extend it to others.*

Healing began with one thought, one belief, one changed behavior at a time until I gradually emerged from the woods into light—and hope—grateful for my sojourn through the wilderness of depression and keenly aware that it was time.

Time for someone with fresh vision and untapped energy to lead.

Time to work with our board and staff members toward a healthy succession plan.

Time to entrust Hope's Promise to another.

Time to retire.

March 2014

It had been two months since Ray and I talked about my retirement vacation in North Carolina. I sat alone on the living room couch, feet propped on the table before me. The setting sun had strewn shadows across the lawn, and the sky dimmed into dusk, then darkness outside the picture window. Our home had plunged into silence on the heels of a whirlwind weekend. Children and grandchildren had arrived from Portland, Kansas City, and Colorado to join agency staff, board members, family, and close friends for my retirement party, hosted by Hope's Promise, at a local country club. Dinner, stories, laughter, presentations, and tears filled the evening. We unwrapped gifts of shared memories that had woven our lives together and stretched through a quarter of a century to mark sacred time.

Gratitude consumed me as I sat in shadowy darkness and listened to the laughter in the walls on that Sunday night. Nourished by weekend memories, my heart was as full as the moon.

Three weeks later we headed for North Carolina: Ray, me, and Annie. Lulled by the soothing rhythm of the tires as we sped down the highway, I leaned in and surrendered to their invitation to lighten my load and embrace unscripted time: no prescribed roles or responsibilities, no playbook, no schedules, and no guarantees.

During our shared journey through marriage, parenting,

adoption, careers, and even my depression, Ray and I had played our roles well. In those crucibles we'd known great love, joy, and sorrow; unearned blessings and unmet expectations; selfishness and selflessness; conflict and reconciliation; laughter and tears; unity and division—parallel tracks of living and loving together in the tension between now and then. Scars and trophies. Children grown. Careers ending. Depression defeated.

Love growing. New season beckoning.

Click-clack. Click-clack. Click-clack thrummed the rhythm of the tires. With each passing mile, I slithered from the constricting responsibility and persona I'd created to escape lifeless skin that no longer fit.

There was nobody I needed to be anymore.

Quiet Reflections

- How have you responded when the realities of life collided with your dreams and expectations? How have your attitudes and behavior impacted your family, loved ones, or work environment?

- Can you describe a time when you felt overwhelmed by life, shamed by your perceived failures, or conflicted with another person? How were, or could, those situations be changed by receiving God's grace and extending it to others?

- Consider the roles you play in your life. Do some no longer fit? Are there others you would like to change? Spend a few moments to honestly share these thoughts and feelings with God.

Chapter 3

Topsail

He stilled the storm to a whisper;
the waves of the sea were hushed.
They were glad when it grew calm,
and he guided them to their desired haven.
Psalm 107:29–30

April 2014, Topsail Island, NC

The beach house that Ray found after days of fiddling on his computer in January felt perfect: a one-of-a-kind, two-story home with panoramic ocean views and thundering surf at high tide that threatened to devour the dune on which it sat. Shelves stuffed with an eclectic assortment of books, shells, and puzzles lined the walls. Cozy furniture with stories to tell invited us to curl up and stay awhile. And the deck, gated and secure, belonged to Annie when she wasn't chasing seagulls on the beach during morning walks with Ray.

At night we walked her together, even in the rain. Halos of mist-infused light encircled streetlamps lining the narrow road behind the house. I yanked the hood of my jacket over my head as we slipped down the back steps, then cowered, resisting the onslaught of rain until finally, I stepped into the downpour.

Wet gravel scrunched beneath our feet as we dodged newly formed puddles in the driveway. Turning left, we headed toward the vacant lot on Seahorse Avenue, where we hoped Annie would quickly relieve herself.

Waiting, soaking wet, with our backs hunched against the rain, we spontaneously stole a sideways glance at each other, then erupted into laughter—drenched heads tossed back with rain streaming down our faces. The absurdity of standing beneath a streetlamp on a deserted island road in the rain, waiting for a puppy to pee, seemed hilarious. At that moment, as belly laughter rippled through my body, it was as if the stress of a quarter century cracked, broke loose, and surrendered to its washing away.

Once we caught our breath, Ray turned to me, warm eyes gazing into mine, and whispered, "I feel like I got the girl back that I married."

His words, the first to touch this tender place that had just been exposed, spoke healing and love, forgiveness and gratitude; words that acknowledged and sang hallelujah for the sacred unraveling beneath the streetlamp; words that breathed "yes!" into our future.

I feel like I got the girl back that I married. Words that gave her back to me too.

We had both done this marriage thing imperfectly. But we were still deeply in love and daring to dream about our future—a shrinking canvas that invited us to create the rest of our story despite a diagnosis that had blindsided us during my preparations to retire and our planning of this first trip to Topsail Island.

December 27, 2013, Colorado

We donned jackets, hats, and gloves for a leisurely walk after our late breakfast: Ray, me, Annie, and seven out-of-town family members who remained after celebrating Christmas with us.

We meandered out the front door and down the country road in front of our home with the speed of a herd of turtles.

We drifted into smaller groups over the course of our two-mile walk on this cool, bright morning—reminiscing, continuing to catch up with each other's lives before some would scatter, once again, to faraway states. Younger ones scurried ahead up the hill. I chatted with my brother and his wife in the middle of the pack while Ray and Annie lagged with Melissa, our daughter-in-law, and our oldest son, Chad, who cradled their infant son in a baby carrier.

A sharp whistle pierced the air. "Hey!" yelled Chad. "Dad fell!"

Another whistle. "Dad's down!"

I spun around to see Ray's still, crumpled body on the dusty road behind me. Melissa, who had dropped to the ground beside him, had already begun CPR. I ran down the hill, skidding on loose gravel and calling his name between murmurs of "Oh no! Oh no!" not knowing if he was dead or alive until I knelt beside him. Slowly, he opened his eyes—large and vacant. A niece called 911. Others shed coats and laid them over Ray or slid them under his head as a pillow. Then we nervously waited for help to arrive.

Paramedics from two volunteer fire departments rounded the corner within minutes, then flew into action. One crouched to take Ray's vitals and hook him up for an EKG as he lay on the ground while the other moved among us, gathering information.

"Did you see what happened?" he asked, searching for clues to what might have caused Ray to collapse and the possible extent of his injuries. "Tell me what you saw," he prodded, taking notes as each of us shared our account of Ray's fall. Though anxious to help, we had little to tell. Everything had happened so fast.

Somewhere into this holy huddle, unnoticed, a third man appeared. He worked for the fire and rescue team, he said, and happened to be in the area on his day off when our call came in. He took the EKG tape from the paramedic on the ground, reviewed the strip, then handed it back to him and pronounced it normal. By now Ray was talking, coherent, and cooperative, but still lying on the ground.

After watching the rescue team lift him onto a gurney and load him into the back of the ambulance, I climbed into the front seat with the driver for the ten-mile ride to the hospital.

Ray had suffered a concussion and a small brain bleed when he fell backward onto his head from a standing position. After nine hours in the emergency room, doctors released him with referrals to a cardiologist and a pulmonologist. "We saw some scarring in his lungs," said someone wearing a white coat. "Interstitial lung disease. You'll want to follow up with that."

This was when we first heard the words that upended our lives, stole our future, and thrust us into the medical orbit of doctor appointments, lab work, tests, procedures, and waiting.

Two months later, in late February, his pulmonologist confirmed the diagnosis: interstitial lung disease—a progressive lung-scarring disease that leads to respiratory failure, a disease that had claimed both our fathers' lives—a disease for which there was no cure or effective treatment. A disease that was a death sentence and a widow maker.

By the time we prepared to leave on our road trip to Topsail Island in April, the shock had subsided, and Ray felt better. Although we carried the weight of his diagnosis with us, we wanted to believe we would still have a few years together.

Although Ray had a terminal diagnosis, his pulmonologist had tried to reassure us. "There's no need to worry," he said. "This could stay dormant for years." We tried not to worry. There would be time for that in the days ahead.

So when Ray got the girl back that he married . . . whoosh! That thrust the first bold brushstroke across our diminished canvas. How many more would we add before the intruder rendered it done?

Although Ray's disease intended to steal his life and our shared future, one thing we knew: Topsail would be a significant part of whatever time we had left. We agreed to return as often as we could for as long as we could. This island had quickly become not just another beach, but our happy place, a haven. Like a missing puzzle piece that, once found, completes the picture: beach walks, long talks, lunch at Daddy Mac's, and praying together for a shared vision of the time we had left.

On the morning we finished packing to begin our journey home, Ray paused to watch the sun rise over the Atlantic from the picture window in the master bedroom and wistfully said, "I feel like I'm leaving home."

I would reflect on his words countless times in the months and years to come. But that morning we were headed home to Colorado, into a life marked not by work, striving, schedules, meetings, or projects, but by unstructured time and a great unknown.

There's no need to worry. This could stay dormant for years.

We desperately wanted to believe that. Yet the enormity of this disease began to lay itself down during our island stay, creating palpable tension between knowing that Ray was dying and embracing what time we had—opposites that must now coexist, for a limited time, through conflicting realities.

We had done our best. The storm had calmed to a whisper; the waves of threatening fear hushed. And Ray and I got the girl back that he had married.

While we never asked God to cure Ray, we did pray that he would slow the progression of Ray's disease and give us more time. How will he answer? we wondered as we loaded the car in early May after our month at the beach and then headed for home. We didn't have long to wait.

May–December 2014, Colorado

Over the next few months, we yielded to the rhythms of doctor appointments and medical procedures: two cataract surgeries, one bronchoscopy, lung function tests, and chest x-rays that showed increased scarring. Ray's disease was on the move.

During the in-between spaces created by inherent waiting, we continued to downsize, shedding years of possessions acquired in the raising of seven children as we prepared to move into a smaller house. We sold our family home on five acres and settled into our "retirement cottage" in October. We claimed a simpler life, just the two of us, though our youngest daughter, Abby, who attended college in Oregon, joined us for summers and holidays.

As Christmas drew near, Ray's health plummeted; he was coughing more and feeling weak.

It was time to worry.

I called Ray's primary doctor, but she was sick and unavailable. Unable to reach his pulmonologist, I drove Ray to urgent care. "I'm sorry," said the receptionist, "but there's a two-hour wait. Would you like me to put your name on our list? You can wait here, or come back," she added.

"No, but thank you," I said. Then turning to Ray: "Let's go to the hospital. Someone needs to see you now."

I called his pulmonologist one more time as we drove to the emergency room. "There's no need to go to the ER," the doctor said after I explained the situation and our current plan. "I know what's wrong with him. He has pneumonia. I can just prescribe an antibiotic and save you the hospital costs." Never questioning his diagnosis, we turned around, stopped to pick up the meds, and went home.

Even as we celebrated a subdued Christmas with our family, his condition worsened.

Though Ray came downstairs for breakfast on December 27,

he continued to cough and had little energy. His legs hurt. He wanted to rest, so he slowly, painfully climbed the stairs to our second-story bedroom. As he sat on the side of our bed, trying to catch his breath, I called his pulmonologist.

"I'm worried about Ray," I said. "He's been on the antibiotics and prednisone you prescribed, but he's not getting better. He's very short of breath after any exertion. And this morning both of his legs have started to hurt. He can hardly walk."

"Go ahead and take him to the ER," his doctor said. "He could have blood clots."

After we checked in at the reception desk, Ray eased into a wheelchair. Attendants whisked him into the triage room, where a team worked to take his vitals, document his symptoms, ask clarifying questions, and order x-rays. While we waited, one talkative tech speculated that Ray could have blood clots in his legs, but then again, he doubted that. "We almost never see anyone with blood clots in both legs," he concluded.

Ray had blood clots in both legs and his lungs. He was admitted to ICU with pneumonia (based on the doctor's previous diagnosis that had not been confirmed), atrial fibrillation, interstitial lung disease, and blood clots. Doctors hovered and talked code in hushed voices as they blasted his body with IV drugs.

Our pastor arrived for support and to pray with us. Then, tearing up, he hugged us and left.

"Hey," I said when Ray and I were finally alone, "Do you realize what day it is? We spent last December 27 at the hospital. Remember?"

He did.

"Do you think we could make some different plans for next year?" I asked, bending to kiss him.

"Yes," he agreed. "That would be a good idea."

Ray stayed in the ICU for ten days, his body hosting a perfect storm: blood clots in both legs and his lungs, interstitial lung disease, irregular labs, and a heart gone wonky. He never did have pneumonia. "His condition is very complex," doctors told us. And his heart had jumped to the top of the health concerns list. The goal in ICU was to keep him alive and find the right pharmaceutical cocktail to stabilize his condition before moving him to a regular hospital room and, eventually, home.

I kept vigil, spending nights in a recliner next to his bed with short breaks to run home, shower, and check the mail. I also wanted to assure the dogs I hadn't abandoned them. Yes, now there were two. Believing Annie needed a canine companion we had gotten Cooper, another standard poodle, who was by then seven months old. Both pups seemed happy; Abby was home for the holidays.

Ray came home on oxygen after twelve days in the hospital, with a fistful of follow-up doctor's appointments. After navigating his slow and fragile recovery, we would adjust our lives and expectations to his new normal. And plan our return to Topsail.

Quiet Reflections

- What people, circumstances, diagnosis, or other unwanted reality has intruded upon your life? How do you feel about that? Where do you believe God was in your story during that time?

- What pieces of you have been lost or left behind on life's journey? Which ones do you want to reclaim? Take a few moments to sit with God and tell him how you feel about this loss. Rest, and be still in this space until your heart settles.

- If your future were a canvas, what picture would you paint? What is the next "brushstroke" you can make? When will you do it?

Chapter 4

Return to Topsail

Although the Lord gives you
the bread of adversity and the water of affliction,
your teachers will be hidden no more. . . .
Whether you turn to the right or to the left,
your ears will hear a voice behind you, saying,
"This is the way; walk in it."
Isaiah 30:20–21

April 2015

We returned to Topsail Island four months after Ray's second hospital stay.

Some mornings, after our walk on the beach, Ray stopped by the local coffee shop. He liked being asked, "The usual?" I think it helped him feel like he belonged. That rarely happened back home, where shifts of bustling baristas hardly noticed and seldom remembered.

Or he'd cruise nearby neighborhoods searching for For Sale signs, trying perhaps to reconfigure a different outcome for what was happening in his body. I've wondered if looking at houses allowed him to envision feeling better longer and our lives unfolding within a ten-minute drive of the beach—our happy place.

I knew what he was doing but couldn't encourage it. I hoped whatever these outings inspired in him would lead to another conclusion. For I, too, was grappling with our shrinking list of options, his dwindling number of days, and the drastically different outcomes we each faced. So I stayed behind on those mornings when he stopped by the Daily Grind for his usual, picked up groceries at Harris Teeter, and collected flyers of homes for sale. He needed that time alone. I did too.

"You know," he said one morning as he walked into the kitchen door and set a small sack of groceries on the counter between us, "I'd really like to move here."

"Wow. Why now?" I asked as he continued to unpack that day's provisions. "It seems so counterintuitive . . . leaving our home, our kids and grandkids, our community, and church family at a time when we're going to need them the most."

"I know," he admitted apologetically as his eyes met mine. "But I can breathe better here. And I want this quality of life for as long as I can."

With those words Ray flung the focal point of his dream for our future onto our unfinished canvas. It was bold, unmistakable. When he stood between the parallel tracks of life and death and followed their trajectory to where they merged into one, I think he saw Topsail Island. The place where we would share life and death. Then life again for both of us.

Ray had had a change of heart earlier in our marriage; he became a "giver" to help my adoption dream come true. Then, after adopting, to say "I give you my blessing" to graduate school and starting Hope's Promise. Now it was my turn. I wanted to bless him. Everything that encompassed a cross-country move—planning, letting go, and following—would be the last thing I could do for him. Our last big adventure.

But still.

"Give me a little time on this one," I said. I felt scattered and needed time for all of me to catch up with myself and occupy the same space at the same time. Not only to sync my thoughts and feelings, but to give myself wholeheartedly to my love for this man while considering the thoughts and feelings of our children.

Later that day I slipped onto the deck overlooking the ocean and called Chad, our oldest son. A test balloon. He answered right away.

"Hey, Mom. Everything okay?"

"Yes. Everything's fine. Have a minute?"

"Sure."

"I want to run an idea by you," I said as my mind formed Ray's request into the shape of a target, then assembled words to nail the bullseye. "Dad and I've been talking," I began. "And he wants to move here. As soon as we can. You know how much better he feels at the beach. But I want to know what you think about it."

He paused, then thoughtfully said, "Mom, if that was me, I hope Missy would do the same thing for me."

Done and done.

All of me in.

I felt reasonably sure the other six would agree.

Standing on that deck a few mornings later, our last one on Topsail before heading home, Ray and I lingered in an embrace. Gazing over the Atlantic, we drank in one last look, hoping it would sustain us through all that awaited us until our return.

May–August 2015
Colorado

Ray had a lung biopsy and hospital stay ten days after we arrived home. The results were devastating—idiopathic pulmonary fibrosis. The worst type of interstitial lung disease.

"What's the prognosis?" one of us asked the surgeon a few

days later as we sat on cold metal chairs in his office to discuss the biopsy results. "Will we have time to move to North Carolina?"

Tight-lipped and noncommittal, he glanced at the nurse beside him, then suggested we discuss the prognosis with Ray's pulmonologist. We pushed. "Well, it's hard to know," he conceded, pausing to carefully choose his next words. "But I'd say you have anywhere from six months to . . . well, I've seen someone live ten years after this diagnosis," he concluded.

Assuming Ray's expiration date would fall somewhere between these outside predictions, we forged ahead, trying to rearrange our uncertain future within a ticking clock.

"What if you knew you had a year to live," I asked a few days later. "Would you move?"

"Absolutely!"

"How about a few weeks?"

"Probably not."

Trying to quantify the worth of our dream against its cost, we played the what-if game, shaving increments of time from both ends of the spectrum until we arrived at six months. Yes, we agreed. We would move for six months. That seemed like a safe bet, and we were praying—not that God would heal Ray but that he would give us more time together and some positive medical news every now and then.

In retrospect, deciding to move was the easy part. Getting to North Carolina, however, proved more challenging.

Our daughter Sarah got married at the end of May. When Ray took the floor to dance with her, a portable oxygen concentrator slung over his shoulder and a canula in his nose, the room wept. I grieved for what was to come, and for another daughter who would never dance with her daddy on her wedding day.

Ray's mother died on our anniversary, three days later. After getting airline-approved medical equipment and a doctor's letter for Ray to fly, we booked our flights to Portland to join his family and mourn his mother's death within the shadow of his own.

Back home, my mother's health continued to deteriorate. She suffered from transient ischemic attacks (TIAs), or mini-strokes; nosebleeds; and heart disease. Telling her we planned to move, just two years after moving her from Kansas to Colorado to be near our family, had been painful. I would rethink our decision to move countless times, yet I always reached the same conclusion: I wanted to move for Ray.

Anxious to get our downsized home on the market and be on our way, Ray and I scrambled to complete the home improvement projects we had begun the previous October when we moved in. His December hospital stay and subsequent long recovery had forced us to put them on hold. The recent biopsy report, however, compelled us to finish them as quickly as possible. Yet amid a booming real estate economy and worker shortages, delays mounted. The crowning blow came when a hailstorm pummeled the roof, our newly finished basement flooded, and the roofing contractor disappeared. Poof. Gone.

Although overwhelmed and discouraged, Ray continued to wet vac the basement and call other construction workers, whose wait lists dragged into months. "I'm afraid we're never going to make it to North Carolina," he lamented one afternoon—the first hint of despair I'd seen since his diagnosis.

"You know what?" I said. "Just a minute . . ."

I ran to the kitchen, yanked the calendar off the wall, and sat down beside him on the couch. "Okay. We just need to get there," I said as I flipped to August and pointed to that day's date on the calendar. "Let's pick a date," I said, skimming through the weeks with my finger. "How about Labor Day? It's a little over three weeks away. Let's get there by Labor Day." I was on a roll—in my element, Point A to Point B with spreadsheets. Ray smiled. We needed to get on with our last big adventure.

And so we did.

Together we conquered logistics—five pages worth: moving estimates, contracts, packing dates, selling real estate and cars, flying to North Carolina to find a home, saying goodbye to family and friends, keeping medical appointments for Mom and Ray, meeting with our children about taking over Mom's care, and finalizing roof and basement repairs. But I faced my private challenge alone.

It had no line, box, or completion date to check; it was the one that roiled and grew like dark, tumultuous clouds, hovering, threatening until they spilled what they couldn't contain on whatever was in their path. Anticipatory grief refused to Just. Go. Away.

It began with crying—alone in the car or in the shower. Sometimes at night, after Ray had gone to sleep, I'd slip out of bed and into my office, sit behind closed doors, and sob. Big, gulping, muffled sobs that sucked air and gorged on fragile emotions and fear.

Then I began to write—a journal for this dying season. A place to spill what I could not contain. A way to harness the tornado brewing in me and funnel it onto a page. These words, legible symbols of my inner storm, held the anger and frustration of unanswered prayers. The myriad thoughts and emotions of knowing my husband and mother were dying plunged and pooled on the page. Selling our home and leaving family and friends was painful. I understood that while we were moving cross country as a couple, I would return alone. I feared what was to come in that in-between time. If depression had brought hopelessness and despair, how would I ever survive the overwhelming grief of Ray's death?

Quiet Reflections

- Have you experienced the "bread of adversity" and "water of affliction?" (Isaiah 30:20–21). How did you respond to these challenges? Where did you find relief?

- What parallel tracks do you see racing through your life? How do you live with the tension these two realities create?

- What has been your response to grief and loss in your life? Jesus, a man of sorrow and suffering, has great compassion for us in our grief. Take a few moments to quiet your mind and your heart. Close your eyes and breathe deeply. Now imagine Jesus calling you by name and offering His comfort to you. What do you notice? How do you feel?

Part Two

Setting Sail

*I will lead the blind by ways they have not known,
along unfamiliar paths I will guide them;
I will turn the darkness into light before them
and make the rough places smooth.
These are the things I will do;
I will not forsake them.*
Isaiah 42:16

Passing Through

I have summoned you by name; you are mine.
When you pass through the waters,
I will be with you; and when you pass through
the rivers, they will not sweep over you.
Isaiah 43:1b–2a

August 28—September 5, 2015, North Carolina

On Tuesday, when Ray and I turned out of our Colorado driveway for the last time, we knew where this road would end. But along the way, we prayed for more time together and hoped for happy memories. The house we had found on a quick trip to North Carolina three weeks earlier felt like home when we rolled into the driveway on Friday night.

We unloaded the car, introduced Cooper and Annie to their new home and yard, then cooked a frozen pizza from the nearby Harris Teeter supermarket for dinner. After settling the dogs for the night, we tackled our own sleeping arrangements, laughing as we tossed inflatable air mattresses and bedding from home on the bedroom floor. Although far from luxury accommodations, it did feel adventurous. Exhausted, we turned out the lights and fell asleep to the hissing and thumps of Ray's oxygen concentrator and doggie snores.

A beautiful organic fruit basket arrived on our porch the following morning. "Blessings on this next step," read the enclosed card, "and we all look forward to sharing this new journey with you. Your kids."

But it would be days before our furniture arrived. In the meantime, we shuffled two lawn chairs between living room, patio, and beach. We delighted in our morning coffee rituals, at home or at the Daily Grind, after a walk on the beach. And we felt grateful that Ray now lived untethered from his oxygen for most of the day. We cooked simple meals with limited supplies, eating off two plates on an upended suitcase we used as our table. Each evening we settled into the chairs on the patio after dinner to watch pine trees dance in the woods beyond our backyard fence as the sun slipped through their branches and set on another day.

Tuesday, September 1

"Let's go for a picnic on the beach tonight!" I said, talking fast as I spun into action. "We'll take a bottle of wine, a simple dinner, and our chairs! It'll be fun."

Ray grinned. He knew it was a good idea. He also knew trying to stop or change it would be like spitting in the wind. Useless and messy.

I grilled chicken, unaware that this ordinary task was the onramp to assuming Ray's other responsibilities I would soon need to deal with. For now, it was a small pivot. Ray had been the family grill master, though not a particularly good one. He preferred conversation around the grill while flipping burgers until they shrank and rivaled the size and mass of a hockey puck, to the actual art of grilling. "The well-done ones are on this side," he would say with a smile, pointing to the plate in his hand as he set the burnt offering on the table with the rest of the meal. He lost his grilling privileges when he was put on oxygen.

Driving over the bridge from the mainland later that afternoon, we saw Topsail Island through different eyes. We weren't tourists anymore. We had come here to live out our uncertain future: one that began with a diagnosis that changed the trajectory of just about everything. Picnics couldn't wait. Our bare feet hit the sand minutes later.

We parked; grabbed food, wine, and chairs; kicked off our shoes; and trudged through deep, shifting sand to find a perfect spot. "It still feels like we're on vacation, doesn't it?" I asked while setting up our chairs and laying out the meal. "But we're not! We can do this every day." *For a while,* I thought. *Until the hard stuff hits.* I squeezed back tears as we poured wine into plastic cups and toasted our good fortune.

"On what day did God create the ocean?" I asked, breaking companionable silence a short time later as we nibbled dinner from paper plates near the water's edge.

"Not sure," Ray said, setting aside his meal and tugging his phone from the pocket of his shorts. I waited while he scrolled through the text of a Bible app. "The third day," he said.

"Read it to me . . ."

And so he did, as the song of the ocean sang its timeless lament just for us. I listened as he recounted the story of creation in the first chapter of Genesis: "God called the dry ground 'land,' and the gathered waters he called 'seas.' And God saw that it was good . . . and there was evening, and there was morning—the third day" (Genesis 1:10, 13).

Warm ocean breeze and toes nestled beneath the surface of sand's gritty weight anchored me in the story. I listened to Ray's steady voice above the murmur of gentle waves uncurling themselves onto the beach and then retreating, over and over again.

The soothing, repetitive sound evoked thoughts of days unfolding and retreating through one generation after another until these waves found us here.

Familiar words from Scripture washed over me as Ray continued to read. Yet that evening they rearranged themselves, adjusting the posture of my soul as I absorbed their meaning from this ocean that had ebbed and flowed through generations of created time.

God cradles our story, from beginning to end, within his own. We are just passing through. I found comfort in the company of saints in this universal perspective. God had not singled Ray and me out for a unique loss; we shared in one that is common to all. The personal sorrow to come, however, was what scared me.

My struggle to accept suffering was about to escalate as Ray's condition worsened. A looming crisis of faith would wrap my soul in tattered garments of unanswered prayer and silence a beggar's plea. It would take an honest encounter with Jesus and a surrendering of my will before I could begin to reconcile my pain with my concept of a loving God.

But that night, after our picnic on the beach, Ray and I watched in silence as the ocean relinquished its blues and greens and quietly surrendered to a fiery orange of day's retreat.

Grateful for another day, we gathered our things and drove home.

Thursday, September 3

Ray drove to Wilmington and bought two more lawn chairs, air mattresses, and bedding. Only the finest for my brother, Jeff, and his wife, Linn, who arrived the following day for an overnight stay. They were on a month-long motorcycle trip that would take them up the East Coast into Canada and back to their home in Oklahoma. The four of us lounged on the beach, dined at Daddy Mac's, and shared snacks, stories, and laughter around our suitcase table. I cherished their love and support while remembering what a neighbor had told Ray and me with a chuckle when we met him on a walk around our new neighborhood: "When you live near the beach, you get lots of company." I was grateful for both.

Saturday, September 5

Our furniture arrived. The eighteen-wheeler lumbered into our neighborhood and eased itself to a stop in front of our home as Ray and I finished our morning coffee. We strolled to the curb to greet two men when they climbed from the cab of their truck on a hot, humid, cloudless morning. Yes, they had the right address. Of course we'd be happy to help.

They found a card table and chair among our belongings and set them up in the shade of the garage. Ray became the gatekeeper. With a roster of several pages spread before him, he checked off each numbered item coming from the truck before movers carried it into the house. There, I directed the flow. This sequence continued throughout the day until boxes filled rooms and ragged sheets of ripped cardboard from unpacked mattresses and mirrors consumed the garage.

Ray's oxygen needs inched upward throughout the day. He was exhausted when the movers left late that afternoon but determined to make his scheduled two-and-a-half-hour trip to Raleigh later that evening; our three sons were coming from Denver to go fishing with their dad. Ray showered and packed an overnight bag, moving slowly to conserve energy. He stopped frequently to catch his breath—a noticeable difference from previous days. Although concerned, I knew how important this trip was to him and that he had the oxygen supplies he needed. Ray assured me he would be fine as we walked to the car.

"Let me know the minute you've got the boys," I said, hugging him goodbye. He promised he would. I waved and blew kisses as he backed from the driveway and drove out of sight, knowing this last fishing trip had been in the making for over three decades.

Quiet Reflections

- "I have summoned you by name; you are mine" (Isaiah 43:1b). What is your response to this declaration from God? How does knowing this fit, or not, with your perspective of God? Of suffering?

- Think of a time when you experienced deep sorrow. Where do you believe God was during that time? How did you deal with that personal pain?

- What did it, or would it, mean for God to be with you when you passed through the waters (Isaiah 43:1–2)? Regardless of what your experience has been, be honest with God about this question. Tell him where you are and what you need.

Fishing

If I fished only to capture fish,
my fishing trips would have ended long ago.
Zane Gray

Write, therefore, what you have seen,
what is now and what will take place later.
Revelations 1:19

I have seen the beginning and the end of fishing trips, but never the during.

I have seen grocery lists scribbled on scraps of paper. Duffel bags carelessly crammed with a clean change of clothes. Maybe a toothbrush. Never a razor. I have seen cardboard boxes filled with firewood. I have seen sleeping bags and a tent, rods, reels, and tackle boxes. And I have seen father and son wave goodbye as they drove down the driveway into their adventure.

A day or two later I have seen them return: mud-caked jeans and smelly socks spilling from duffel bags; half-eaten bags of jumbo marshmallows; empty cardboard boxes save for a scattering of wood chips that swooshed within their borders; and my stubble-cheeked man home from the woods. I have seen wide-faced grins, dirty fingernails, and small gifts they brought to those of us who remained at home.

But I have never seen the during. The sacred ritual of selecting perfect lures, flies, or jigs; scratching meal items off a scribbled list at the grocery store with a stubby pencil that was just the right size for the front pocket of their jeans; chewing bubble gum as they hiked; casting from the shoreline or a wobbly canoe; snagging submerged logs and rarely a fish; roasting hot dogs and marshmallows; and eating beans from a can around the campfire—I have never seen them roll out their sleeping bags, talk in the dark, or pee in the woods.

I have seen the beginning of this tradition—the fruit of countless discussions between Ray and me during our rookie years as parents about values and experiences we wanted to share with our children—traditions we hoped to cultivate throughout their growing-up years.

There were birthday traditions, holiday traditions, and Saturday-morning traditions. Some of our most valued ones grew from individual times with each of our seven children. Several traditions changed along the way, but the purpose did not: to create a strong family grounded in a legacy of faith.

I was a stay-at-home mom for the first fifteen years of our marriage, on-call twenty-four-seven. For better or worse, the kids had me . . . All. Day. Long. But Dad disappeared shortly after they got up, returning home in time for dinner. Although I planned "me and Mom" times with each of them, with varying degrees of success, time alone with Dad was the goal.

When they were young, Ray took our four daughters on "dates." Father-daughter dances at church, a trip to Dairy Queen, or walking the dogs around Palmer Lake. When Abby, our youngest, was fourteen, he called a radio station and won tickets to a concert she wanted to see and then took her. Sometimes he rang the doorbell to pick them up. Other times they stopped for pizza or burgers. "I want them to know how they should expect a young man to treat them," he said. So he showed them.

We decided an overnight father-son fishing trip was a good idea when Chad turned five. Ray launched this adventure with modest objectives and little planning: have fun and bring him safely home. This tradition expanded to include Nick, and then Tyler, when they turned five.

And just like that, it seemed, Ray had three summer fishing trips on his calendar.

As the boys grew, each passing into and (thankfully) out of their version of adolescent rebellion, so did the complexity of Ray's goals for their weekend trips. This may be overstating it for a pretty simple guy who sometimes flew by the seat of his pants. He still wanted to have fun and bring them safely home, but through the years, lingering time around the campfire created space for discussions about birds and bees, manhood, fatherhood, and leadership. Respect earned. Belonging nurtured. Love strengthened. Ray and I always knew these trips weren't about fishing. They were about raising sons.

When little-boy immaturity and attention spans threatened the sustainability of these outings, Ray adapted. They had to camp close enough to civilization so they could drive into town for breakfast. And Ray needed something to do with the boys in the afternoon while the fish slept. That was how Putt-Putt golf became a fishing tradition . . . and stubby pencils filled jean pockets.

When each son turned sixteen, Ray took them on a weeklong fishing trip to the Boundary Waters—a mosaic of a thousand pristine lakes and streams nestled within a million acres of wilderness that straddles the United States and Canadian border between Minnesota and Ontario. Limited civilization and no Putt-Putt golf. By then, however, it *was* more about the fishing.

As boys grew into men, individual fishing trips with their dad evolved into a foursome that pilgrimaged together: a float trip down the John Day River in Oregon; fishing Gold Lake in the Sierras, Red Feather Lake near Estes Park, and trips to various watering holes in Medicine Bow National Forest in Wyoming, the Colorado and Yampa Rivers, and their favorite pond at Fish and Cross Ranch.

When Tyler got engaged, he didn't want a bachelor party, he said. He preferred to go fishing with his dad and brothers. So Ray rented a remote cabin with a pond and a view. They shopped for groceries, picked out perfect lures, and then went fishing. Instead of Putt-Putt golf while the fish slept, they shared a beer and watched the sun set from a rustic deck and read the letters of wit and wisdom they had written for Tyler.

I have seen the beginning, and the end, of countless fishing trips over the years. But I have never seen the during.

Stories? Yes. I've heard many. I've seen them through the eyes of my heart and my imagination and my knowing of these four men—father and sons with children of their own. Grown men, diverse in temperament, goals, politics, and spiritual beliefs. How they bonded while fishing and argued over beer. How they sought to both help and change each other and, over time, how they grew to respect one another for the men they had become.

"Kids tend to befriend creeks the way adults befriend one another: start shallow, and slowly work your way deeper," said David James Duncan in his memoir *My Story as Told by Water*.[5] Through the years our boys befriended not only creeks and one another in this way, but, I suspect, also themselves.

By the time he was diagnosed with interstitial lung disease, Ray had been fishing with his boys for more than thirty-five years.

That was when we all began working our way into deeper waters.

"Mom," said one son, "we want to take Dad on one last fishing trip. It's been a couple of years since our last one." He was speaking on behalf of his brothers sometime after Ray and I decided to move to North Carolina but were mired in the delays of getting there. "Whaddya think?"

"I think it's a great idea . . . but you better hurry."

That Father's Day Ray opened an empty photo album and a card from all three boys that explained their fishing trip gift. They would plan it together and fill the album with pictures. But where could they go? Ray was now on oxygen full time and had limited stamina for anything more than what would be required for getting around the house or going on short errands.

"Mom, what about . . ." one son would ask, filling in the names of various Colorado places they had fished and camped as he went down the list.

"The elevation's too high," I said about the first. "There's no phone reception or electricity for his oxygen concentrator." Or "It's too far from a hospital," I replied to others, torpedoing each suggestion. "But you better hurry," I added.

"What about the Boundary Waters?" Ray asked. Off they went on that tangent until he realized that his declining health had nixed that one too.

In the end, we decided the boys would fly to North Carolina for an extended weekend trip a few days after we moved there. Ray would meet them in Raleigh on Saturday after their late flight and spend the night there before he brought them back to our home on Sunday. They would drive to Virginia on Monday to visit and fish with Ray's sister, Joanne, who lived on a lake. It was a modified plan that replaced jumbo marshmallows, mountain streams, and Putt-Putt golf with electrical outlets, home cooking, and access to medical care.

This was how it came to be that I was waving goodbye to Ray on Saturday evening after the moving truck had left. He was on his way to Raleigh to pick up our three grown sons for the beginning of their last fishing trip.

In keeping with tradition, I did not see the during. But I would see the end.

Quiet Reflections

- What role have traditions played in your life, marriage, family, or work relationships? How did that change with the loss of your loved one? What role would you like traditions to play in your future?

- List any traditions you had, or planned to have, that went away with your loved one. Name what you have lost. Imagine being with Jesus and handing him your loss, and your feelings about that loss, to carry for you. Where are you? What do you notice?

- Ray's fishing trips weren't just about fishing with his boys. They were about building relationships. Think of one tradition in your life. In what way could that tradition be used to build relationships with others and with God?

Hours to Live

Your eyes saw my unformed body;
all the days ordained for me were written
in your book before one of them came to be.
Psalm 139:16

September 6–11, 2015, North Carolina

I ran to meet the car as four doors flew open and Ray, Chad, Nick, and Tyler crawled out. Each of them swallowed me in a hug before I steered them into our home cluttered with moving boxes, furniture set in mostly the right places, and lunch.

Our sons were eager to help, so we put them to work. They unpacked boxes, assembled beds in spare bedrooms so they would have places to sleep, and reorganized the garage. All agreed we had found the perfect house.

That evening we dined on the deck at Daddy Mac's overlooking the beach. We shared a long, leisurely meal—to which I felt lucky to be invited since it was the official beginning of their fishing trip. I was grateful it wasn't hot dogs and beans from a can.

We strolled barefoot on the beach after dinner, the boys and I slowing to match Ray's pace. He needed his oxygen that day and carried the portable concentrator on his shoulder as we drifted down the beach. We paused every few steps, intuitively circling around Ray, a gesture both claiming and protective, as we continued our casual conversation. We stood on wet, cool sand where land meets ocean as gentle, lapping waves scurried over our feet and then raced back out to sea. A salty breeze and low-flying gulls reminded us we weren't in Colorado anymore. We snapped pictures of Ray and the boys, each with him, and with both of us—final fishing trip pictures to fill the pages of Ray's Father's Day album—until the sun fell beneath the horizon, pulling the last splinters of light down with it. Although not feeling well, Ray enjoyed the evening and was quiet and content.

Back home, I kissed him good night and then went to bed to read while the guys settled themselves in the living room. Though absent the campfire, they fell into easy conversation as if it were flickering before them. Low murmurs, punctuated by bursts of laughter and comfortable pauses, seeped through the adjoining wall to nourish my mother's heart. This was sacred ground across which an invisible, wordless baton had passed; this time, our sons established the objectives for the time with their dad. They had come prepared to guide the narrative with questions, words of affirmation, and a tape recorder. But they wouldn't be able to bring him safely home.

I was still awake when Ray slipped into bed beside me later that night. "How was it?" I asked.

"I felt so honored," he whispered with tears in his voice. I nestled my head beside his on his pillow as he told me why.

Ray still did not feel well when the four of them left the following morning for his sister's home in Virginia. Although concerned, none of us thought he shouldn't go. He had done well, going for long stretches of time without his oxygen, until recently. And I reminded myself that his doctor had given our move to North Carolina a thumbs-up just a few days earlier when we met with him before leaving Colorado. Everything had looked as good as it could for a dying man.

Memories of that morning, like a comma in a sentence, invite me to pause: What if they hadn't gone? What if Ray had received medical treatment sooner? But I can't go there. Nothing would have changed the outcome, maybe not even the timeline. "All the days ordained for me were written in your book before one of them came to be."

Did Ray know how sick he was when he left that day? I think he might have understood more than he shared with us. Leaving town to go fishing with his sons might not have been the only right answer for how to spend his last days, but I'm certain it would have ranked toward the top of his list.

Ray and I knew their fishing trips weren't about fishing.

Like all the other fishing trips over the past thirty-five years, I have seen the beginning but not the during. Unlike the others, however, I did get updates.

Monday, September 7: Texts with Ray
3:09 p.m.

> Ray: *Arrived safely.*
> Me: *Good. Thx for letting me know. How are you breathing on 1–10?*
> Ray: *8. Pretty consistent oxygen level around 91.*
> Me: *And how are you feeling overall?*
> Ray (two hours later): *Just got off the boat from before dinner fishing. Walked up the hill with 4 stops. Not too bad.*

Tuesday, September 8: Texts with Ray
5:24 a.m.

> Me: *Good morning. How did you sleep? And how do you feel?*
> Ray: *Rough night. Couldn't get oxygen to stay above 88. Cold. Let the boys go fishing with Jo and I stayed in bed. Better now. You?*
> Me: *I'm sorry! Don't forget you have the extra tanks that will give you more than 4 liters. . . . I'm fine.*

Wednesday, September 9

Joanne stayed behind with Ray this morning while the boys left early to fish. She texted me around eight, igniting a series of texts and events:

Me to all three boys: *Dad is not doing well. You need to get back and get him here ASAP.*

Nick: *Reeling in now. We'll be headed back shortly.*

Me: *Good. I'm calling dr. now, making plans for ER. Dad is on extra tanks. They won't last long. You will be going to New Hanover Regional Medical Center.*

Chad: *Didn't this change to Duke?*

Me: *Possibly. I think it should. Tyler said you would discuss it in the car once you left there. Let me know ASAP.*

Chad: *Mentioned Duke with Dad, he wants to see how his oxygen use is.*

Chad: *Confirming Duke University Hospital.*

Me: *Good. I've made arrangements to board dogs . . . You will probably beat me there. Keep me posted all the way . . . Go to ER. Make sure they know his CO doc told him to go and that he will speak with them about dad's history and present situation.*

Chad (11:58): *Got here about 10 mins ago, Dad being seen now.*

Ray went through triage once they arrived at the hospital in Durham, North Carolina. The four of them were sitting in the ER waiting room when I arrived from our home two hours later. Doctors finally called him to an exam room five hours after he'd first been seen. I went with him. Outside, three sons wrestled with what to do. Should they stay or leave as planned?

"I think it's fine for each of you to go home," I told them later. "You've had a few days together with Dad that meant so much to him. I'm sure he'd want you to go. He knows you have families and jobs that need you. Nobody here seems overly concerned at this point." Because Ray had been in and out of the hospital several times over the past eighteen months, this felt routine. "I expect they'll keep him long enough to get his medications and oxygen stabilized. I'll be sure to let you know if anything changes," I added.

Deciding to leave, yet unsettled with their decision, they came, one at a time, to tell Ray goodbye before catching their flight to Denver.

Ray moved into a hospital room later that evening. During another rough night, as medical staff scuttled in and out trying to fix various machines that were attached to Ray, I dozed in spurts beside his bed.

Thursday, September 10:

Ray started to run a fever. His oxygen needs climbed. Doctors ordered tests. A nurse assured me that everything was stable, and yes, it would be fine for me to get a good night's sleep at a nearby hotel. Expecting Ray to be hospitalized for several days, I made the reservation. I hoped to sleep well in a bed before spending a string of nights in a chair.

Friday, September 11:
6:47 a.m.

Ray: *Will be moving to ICU in an hour or so.*

Me: *On my way.*

Ray had just arrived in the intensive care unit when I hurried to his bedside a few minutes later.

Crossing that threshold, I slid, like Alice, down the rabbit hole. Nothing was as it should be in this altered reality. Everything was moving, shifting, inside and out, surreal. The scenes before me played out in slow-motion images with filtered, muted edges—doctors floating into the room as white coattails followed, whispering conspiratorially with one another, then drifting back out, sympathetic nurses tending beeping machines.

Until I knew.

Within seconds of entering his room, hopes shattered. Numbing fog disappeared, lifting its mantel of protection to expose an intensity that both magnified and minimized everything within these walls: Ray's critical condition hung in the sacred space of few words. We had expected his disease to progress incrementally, his need for oxygen increasing as fibrous growth in his lungs claimed more territory.

Nothing had prepared me for this explosive acceleration to life threatening within days.

Ray's oxygen needs skyrocketed: fifteen liters. Twenty-five. Two doctors sat with us to compassionately discuss life support, both the option and the process of putting him on a ventilator. Ray and I had first talked about this decision months ago and had periodically revisited the issue. He had consistently said no, he did not want life support.

That was hypothetical. This was real.

"What are his chances of being able to come off the ventilator?" I asked.

"About ten percent," replied a white coat with sad eyes.

We thanked the doctors as they rose to leave. Then we waited several hours before deciding what to do, praying the antibiotics would work. As time ran out, doctors pressed for our answer.

"Sweetheart, this is your decision," I said holding his hand and searching his eyes.

"No," he softly said, "this is a 'we' decision."

"I don't think I can make the decision to turn it off," I finally whispered, choking on tears.

"Then our answer is no."

Calm. Gracious. Accepting. Just as he'd been when he heard his diagnosis; when he endured painful procedures; and when, that morning, he texted to say, "Will be moving me to ICU."

Stepping from his room a few minutes later, I walked down the hall to the waiting room, where I called my sister, Kristi. She lived three hours away in Virginia. Her bags were packed. "I need you to come now," I said. "I really need you here. Joanne's coming too. And I'm calling the kids after I hang up with you."

Then, one by one, I phoned each of our seven adult children in Oregon, Missouri, and Colorado. I had rehearsed what I would say, trying to ensure each one heard the same message. News traveled swiftly between them on the grapevine they had perfected through the years. I didn't want any misunderstandings.

After giving what I hoped was a calm, accurate update on Ray's condition, I paused to let them absorb the news and then answered their questions. I concluded each call, as gently as I could, with this: "If you want to see Dad before he dies, you need to get here as quickly as you can."

They all arrived the next day. Some made it before he died; others did not.

Ray was conscious, relatively comfortable, and able to have short conversations throughout Friday. Visits with Kristi and his sister, Joanne, who had both arrived from Virginia that afternoon, touched him. He talked or texted with others: our children who were on their way, his brother, Larry, and Corbin, our fifteen-year-old grandson who, as a toddler had given us our grandparent names of Bum and Mimi. Ray texted Corbin that he "only had a few hours to live." He encouraged him to "Decide now the person you want to be. Pick the path every day how to get there and fight daily to stay on that path. Love you, Bum."

Neither one of us slept that night in the ICU. We understood that Ray was dying; the next medical intervention would be a morphine push when he needed it. The beginning of the end. Despite Ray's looming death, I felt an unexpected sense of calm alongside my grief in the waiting. It was not defeat, resignation, or denial—but an acceptance of what was to come because God is God, and I am not. This fragile surrender was grace for that night. But the training ground had been painful. It had begun years ago with depression and reemerged as a more recent crisis of faith.

Quiet Reflections

- Think of a time when you were tempted to second-guess an important decision you had made. What was your response? How do you handle the what-ifs of life? How did you make peace with that decision?

- If faced with the life support decision, do you know what your spouse, your children, or your parents would choose? Do they know your wishes on this question? When would be a good time to talk about this with them?

- If you could write one last text to someone, who would it be and what would it say?

Crisis of Faith

Teach me your way, LORD,
that I may rely on your faithfulness;
give me an undivided heart,
that I may fear your name.
Psalm 86:11

Fall 2007, Colorado

Four words nailed my story: *She tried really hard. They should be chiseled on my gravestone*, I thought one afternoon as I dragged myself home from work. I was sopped up and wrung out. Life had sucked me dry. I didn't want to die; I just wanted to stop hurting, to disappear, to somehow not be here. I couldn't see beyond a life that extracted my daily energy quota just to crawl out of bed each morning. I had fought back for a very long time, crippled by inadequate tools and a voice from my past that had worn out its welcome: A quitter never wins, and a winner never quits.

Until she does.

I hung my keys on a hook by the kitchen door, dropped my purse and briefcase on the counter, walked downstairs to an extra bedroom at the far end of the house, and slipped into bed. Pulling the covers over my head, I scrunched beneath them and prayed they would make me invisible. Asking to please be left alone, I stayed there all night. Undone. Overwhelmed.

I *had* tried really hard. It wasn't enough, but it was my wake-up call.

"Suffering is a reality that demands our full attention," says author and friend Esther Lovejoy.[6] I was responsible for much of my pain, given the image I had created and worked hard to maintain.

Exhaustion, striving's toxic waste and the source of my unraveling as I lay beneath those covers, had finally slung me into the abyss of depression. Although painful for a season, it was not a final destination but, rather, a merciful gift inviting me to encounter Jesus in my brokenness and to exchange the lies I had come to believe for God's truth. I would, however, need to go back before I could move forward.

After that undone and overwhelming night, I began to meet with Carol, a professional counselor. In addition to learning about grace, I allowed her to gently guide me back into my childhood to discover the wound that had led me to create defense mechanisms, or my "little-girl tools," that had led to my exhaustion.

Whenever we met, Carol and I invited the Holy Spirit to guide us. During one session he led us to a bright, sunny afternoon when I was about five years old. My dad was pushing me on a swing in our backyard. Higher and higher I went until I fell and got hurt. I needed a hug but got back on the swing instead. Dad didn't mean to hurt me. My fall was an accident, and he and I had been having fun. This would have been an insignificant incident except for what I began to believe that afternoon. *Whenever I get hurt, I must minimize the pain and move on.* I wanted to avoid the rejection I feared would come from my dad if I cried or complained.

I perfected my little-girl tool of "minimize and move on" as I matured. This strategy left many thoughts and feelings unvalidated and unresolved, although additional facts would later substantiate why I had come to develop it in the first place.

My mother told me, when I was an adult with children of my own, that Dad did not visit me or her during the five days we remained in the hospital after my birth because I was a girl and not a boy. Years later, long after my parents had divorced, I would learn that they had separated for several months after I was born. And that my mother and I went to live with my grandparents in another state.

That information was hurtful. I resented that it had been kept a secret for decades. But it did explain why I grew up feeling like I had to earn my father's approval, even when I fell off a swing. It also lent insight into the image I had created over the years to mitigate the possibility of failure and rejection. I became a tenacious, unflappable achiever, able to manage what life dished out: rebellious teenagers, a daughter with mental illness who rejected me as her mother, graduate school with five children, and a stressful career.

Counseling helped me understand and own my responses to the events of my life and not blame my dad. He had been an involved father and a positive role model for me in many ways. I knew that Dad, deeply wounded by the suicidal death of his own father when he was young, had done the best he could. The day before he died, as we visited by his bedside, Dad told me he was an agnostic but that he "saw no evidence of God." This perspective had made it impossible for him to understand or respect the importance of my faith, or why I would start a nonprofit Christian organization, or adopt children from different races.

Moments before I walked into his bedroom to have what would be my last conversation with my father in the summer of 2013, I spoke with Ray on the phone; he was home in Colorado. "Sweetheart, would you please consider asking him for his blessing?" he gently asked.

"No, I won't," I replied, saddened by my response. "That ship has sailed. I'm okay. I don't need his blessing. Besides, he would have no idea what I was talking about." I loved my father and was grateful for the countless positive ways he had shaped my life and supported my family. I had accepted what he could and could not provide.

September 2015, North Carolina

Bad news stuck to us like a drunken tattoo. Doctors scratched their heads and dubbed Ray their "science project" as his health continued to deteriorate despite their best efforts. Meanwhile, I felt as if my recent retirement, our empty nest, and a cross-country move had conspired to rob me of significant roles and support systems but left nothing in return. Quietly, without thought or resistance, old habits that had contributed to my earlier depression hijacked my fear of failure in the face of Ray's impending death. If I tried harder. If I prayed more fervently. If I meticulously prepared low-sodium meals and helped regulate Ray's blood-sugar levels and researched alternative treatment options, then maybe God would answer with "Yes."

When we didn't receive positive results on medical tests or a slowing of Ray's disease, I began to crater. Fear ravaged old wounds. Relics of unfinished business dangled and came undone, like stray hairs from an updo that's seen a rough night.

I felt betrayed by God. It wasn't that I didn't believe in God. I did. I believed he was good, that he loved me, and nothing could separate me from his love—at least in some abstract, ethereal way. I also believed he could answer prayer. But he wasn't answering mine, not that I could see anyway.

Later, I would connect the miraculous ways that God had unspooled His answer to my deepest prayer through five decades before I had even cried out to him. As time hurled us toward Ray's death, however, I measured God's faithfulness with the short stick of Ray's physical condition and my spiritual one. Both were suffocating. If God didn't answer my prayers, since that was His job, it must be my fault, I reasoned. What if, in this biggest loss of my life, I didn't have what it took? Was I a Christian poser, full of talk with little substance? Would God be enough? I had to know.

My perception and experience of God have changed and matured through the years, influenced by compassionate biblical teaching, like-minded family members and friends with whom I share life, personal study and prayer, and life experiences inherent to aging in a broken world. When I wrestled with my fear of Ray dying, wondering if God would be enough to sustain me and how I would survive the grief, I noticed a "we" faith had woven itself into the fabric of our marriage and me. This was different from, yet enhanced by, my personal faith. As Ray and I lived our everyday lives—loved, worked, argued, made up, played, questioned, served, raised children—this "we" faith, who we were as a Christian couple, had acquired a life and energy all its own—one that required both of us to keep it alive.

Talking with Ray was often easier than praying to God . . . or maybe sharing my heart with him was praying. He listened with his heart and his eyes, hugged me, and tried to fix things gone awry—sometimes when he should have stopped at the hug. I knew he cared, and I'd been heard and not judged. From some place deeper than words, I understood that the physical and spiritual void Ray's death would create terrified me. How much of me, of my faith, would remain when he was gone?

Like any loss, mine was not happening within a vacuum. It came amid the rubble and ruin of deceit. A fragile truce within our extended family had exploded when my father died two years earlier. It still raged. When I felt personally attacked in the aftermath, I got mad. Angry words I once thought myself incapable of saying flew past my lips—words that should have made hair grow on my sweet husband's bald head. Unseemly and unwholesome words, but amazingly satisfying, if only for fleeting tension-relieving moments. This family conflict became the landfill where

I chucked all my anger, even that which stemmed from Ray's disease, allowing me to acknowledge only the grief in his dying. Until my crisis of faith.

Dr. Sanjay Gupta, renowned brain surgeon and health journalist, addressed the function of memory in his article "Quest for Better Brain Health" like this:

> Memories exist to reinforce a person's life's narrative and to create a sense of identity and place in the world. It's part of the reason that memories can be so easily forgotten or contaminated. If they don't fit your life's narrative, they serve far less purpose. Plus, it's why our "memory" of something constantly morphs. As we take in more information, the way we recall past experiences changes how we remember them. This dynamism is partly why it's also true that our memories are not an accurate, objective record of the past.[7]

That explains why I'm not sure my crisis happened exactly this way—only that this is how I remembered it. I am, however, certain of this: the essence of the spiritual, emotional, and internal angst, and the epiphany that calmed me before Ray's death, is as true as I can make it within the boundary of words.

I sat alone in the front seat of my car in the hospital parking lot at Duke Medical Center during Ray's final days in the hospital. Outside my window, tree branches swayed in sync with the breeze as slivers of sunlight twinkled between their leaves. Cloudless skies and warm weather mocked the storm brewing within me, reminding me of life outside my reach as I convened a come-to-Jesus meeting. I then verbally puked residual bile from a gut retched empty, heaving it all at the foot of the cross. I poured out fear of Ray dying and not being able to live without him, frustration with God for not answering my prayers, and anxiety about the state of my relationship with him on the brink of Ray's death. I knew I needed God's help and the faith to trust him, but I had no idea how to right my sinking ship. Time was running out. I had to know if he would be enough. *I had to KNOW.*

Then this verse popped unexpectedly to mind: "Teach me your way, LORD, that I may rely on your faithfulness; give me an undivided heart that I may fear your name." I had memorized Psalm 86:11 weeks earlier. As I recalled it that afternoon, my world tilted just enough. I grabbed hold of those words as if they were a lifeline, and their meaning led me here: God is faithful to his way—not mine. This gentle, gracious answer, spoken into my deepest need, pointed to God's faithfulness. I would find it within my surrender.

Like Jesus in the garden the night he was betrayed, I thought. Knowing what was to come the following day, Jesus went with his disciples to Gethsemane. "Then he said to them, 'My soul is overwhelmed with sorrow to the point of death. Stay here and keep watch with me.' Going a little farther, he fell on his face to the ground and prayed, 'My Father, if it is possible, may this cup be taken from me. Yet not as I will, but as you will'" (Matt. 26:38–39).

Jesus knew his story would take him to the cross. Alone. He surrendered his will to the Father and endured the cross for the joy set before him; he saw life on the other side of pain.

I'd prayed for many cups to be taken from me over the past eighteen months. Begged actually, for both Ray and me. I believe God invites us to be vulnerable and honest with him and tells us to cast our burdens on him. But I got stuck in begging for my way.

When my torrent of words ran dry that afternoon, lifeless and spent at the foot of the cross, I finally understood. I surrendered Ray—not my will but yours be done.

"Nobody surrenders by thinking about it," says Emilie Griffin in *Small Surrenders*. "It's not a matter of weighing alternatives, thinking things through. Surrender happens in a particular time and place, in the desert of our lives, when God lets rivers flow . . . And the prodigal son or daughter comes home."[8]

Teach me your way, Lord. These words changed my perspective within the unfolding of Ray's death and sustained me in the unscripted days to follow. I would experience God's "enough-ness" in surrender—in letting go—in giving back to God what he was allowing to be taken away.

"At times of suffering we have three choices," Esther Lovejoy reminds us. "We can rebel against what has happened to us and become angry and bitter. We can resign ourselves to the inevitable with a sense of helplessness. Or we can yield to the purposes of a loving heavenly Father and discover the sweetness of that surrender . . . Surrender is only possible because of what we know to be true about the One to whom we surrender."[9]

I didn't know what I didn't know until what I knew wasn't enough. My "aha" took root in the fertile soil of crisis: God's faithfulness is inherent to his way, to his character. With this truth God gently began to dismantle inaccurate beliefs, assumptions, and practices and then to replace them with a theology of suffering integrated with the loving character of God.

Lord, teach me your way in this dying and in the living to follow. Bend my heart toward you. Cradle my sorrow within your own that I may rely on your faithfulness, even in this pain.

Quiet Reflections

- Have you ever received a "merciful gift" that came wrapped in pain and brokenness? What was the gift within the suffering? How did you receive it?

- In what ways have you tried to barter with God for a desired outcome to your prayers? What have you learned about God's love and faithfulness, even when the answer seemed to be "No"?

- How has your experience and perception of God changed through the years? What influences contributed to this change? Who is he now?

Going Home

Healing comes in telling the story a thousand times.
—Tricia Lott Williford, the Pen and the Page Retreat

Saturday, September 12, North Carolina

Doctors started the morphine around three in the morning.

The red-eye from Denver delivered some of our crew to North Carolina early Saturday morning. They reached the hospital before seven. One by one they drew close to Ray's bedside: final conversations, tears, hugs, and I-love-yous before relinquishing their place to another.

"How long before the others get here?" Ray asked when they all had left to go to the waiting room and we were alone. Three of our children, from Portland and Kansas City, were on their way.

"Not until about noon," I said, glancing at the clock on the wall. That was four hours away.

"I don't think I can wait," he whispered.

"Sweetheart, you don't have to wait," I said, caressing him, unable to stop the tears that had begun hours before. "It's okay to go. You don't have to wait. You've done everything you could possibly do for all of us."

Nick and Tyler returned to sit with me by his bed. The dying team remained outside our door, scanning monitors, watching through a window, and bending hospital rules to allow our large family to come and go. I clutched the tear-soaked blanket draping my shoulders and stepped aside to take a phone call from our pastor.

Then Tyler: "Mom, I think you need to come now. It's Dad . . ." I rushed to Ray's side and cradled him, whispering final words of love and gratitude as I walked him home.

"The time of death is 9:48," said the doctor from the dying team after she examined his eyes a few minutes later. The love of my life had died, surrendered and unafraid.

I had seen the end.

From the day we first heard "interstitial lung disease" in December 2013, when Ray collapsed on a family walk and ended up in the ER, until Jesus called him home on September 12, 2015, I never saw him angry at God. He was never rude to medical professionals who inflicted pain in their efforts to help. He kept his medical appointments, thanked the professionals regardless of the news they delivered, and did his best to comply with their recommendations. He loved me, his children, their spouses, his grandchildren, and our extended families. To his clients and colleagues, he was a gentleman.

The social worker in me had watched for signs along the way. Surely this introvert of mine was "stuffing" his feelings. I'd read the literature and counseled clients. He couldn't hold it together forever.

"Sweetheart," he once explained with a helpless shrug when I shared my concern, "I don't understand it. I just know that if I didn't cause the problem, and I can't fix it, then I can trust God with it." So he did.

Fifteen days after we drove into our new driveway, Ray was going home.

"I need to go," I said to my sister, Kristi, when I found her in the ICU waiting room after I had met with hospital staff to begin the administration of dying. "I need to go home now."

I left my car in the hospital parking lot for others to drive as we cobbled together a plan to convene at our home, 160 miles away. I climbed into Kristi's car. She drove and listened. I cried and talked as we sped down Interstate 40, the first telling of my story on this healing journey.

My cell phone rang somewhere between Durham and Hampstead. "This is Carolina Donor Services," said a warm voice. Did I want to donate Ray's skin and bones too? she asked. Ray and I hadn't known to discuss that option. He was an organ donor; we both were. I knew his heart and lungs would be useless. But his skin and bones?

"How long do I have to think about this?" I asked.

The faceless female voice tried to be compassionate, but time was of the essence.

"I'm sorry," I said. "I just can't make that decision right now. May I call you back?"

Yes, she said, I could, but it needed to be soon.

I was quite sure how Ray would have answered her question. But he wasn't here, and I wasn't so sure. Not now—in the rawness of loss. Either way, I knew, would be fine with him.

Ray and I had tackled his disease and my impending widowhood straight up. We discussed everything we knew to address in the months following his diagnosis. We met around our dining room table on Saturday mornings, where he tutored me on our finances: passwords, banking, investments, bills, insurance, and where to find the paper files. Although we made these decisions together, he had implemented them. I took notes as he talked, knowing that if I had the information, I could figure it out later. And we discussed dying, death, and burial issues. Ray wanted to be cremated. "But sweetheart," he would add, "I really don't care. Whatever's easiest for you is fine with me."

In the hours before he died, we talked again about these things.

"Are you afraid?" I asked.

"No, not for me," he said. "Just for you and the kids."

"Have you thought of anything you want me to include in your service, like favorite songs?"

He shook his head slowly from his hospital pillow, reiterating our previous discussions: whatever's easiest for you.

Ray and I shared similar beliefs about death: when our body dies, our soul still lives. This flesh-and-bones tent was a gift, one that served a good and holy purpose; but absent our soul it was empty—a cocoon shed as a butterfly receiving new life. If what he left behind could help someone, please, take it, he would have said.

But still. The question had yanked the rug out from under the hypothetical and sent me reeling. I prattled on to Kristi, who listened without offering advice. I hoped my words would miraculously rearrange themselves into the answer I needed within my allotted time. In the end, I made it easy on myself.

Kristi and I arrived at my home by midafternoon. Balmy temperatures, clear skies, and immaculate lawns struck me as misplaced and out of sync—backdrops for someone else's story that had erroneously showed up in mine. Walking to the front door, I noticed a white envelope tucked within its handle. Another mistake, I assumed, since Ray and I had not lived there long enough to know our neighbors. I removed it, stepped inside, and opened a sympathy card with a lovely handwritten note from across-the-street neighbors. It was the first of many expressions of love and support I would receive from this community that welcomed me into their fold.

Although Ray and I had moved to North Carolina for him, by then I knew it was where I was supposed to be, even though I had yet to wonder why. This knowing bestowed an unexpected steadiness to the wobbly, uncertain time—one in which I saw countless examples of grace. My children noticed it too, through circumstances, coincidences, the kindness of neighbors and strangers, and the palpable comfort of the beach. But it would be in the unfolding of the next nineteen months during this set-apart season of my life that I would understand why.

On that day, however, my family and I clung to the present. We hugged and cried as each of my children arrived at a home in which they had never lived—the one Ray and I had shared for two weeks. There was a softness, a gentleness in my gathered tribe that day, made richer by our shared experience of death, bowing to the fragility of life, and our love for the man who taught us this.

We caravanned to the beach late that afternoon to take a memory walk for Ray. We migrated as a leaderless flock down the beach, stooping every few steps to retrieve a stone or shell the ocean had tossed ashore. Our slow-paced rhythm forced us to stay in the moment. Some walked alone, others in small groups, shifting, connecting, holding fast the earth to center us in our up-rooted lives. Someone suggested we collect these treasures from the sea to use in a centerpiece at Ray's service, lending form and function to our walk, our remembering, and our private thoughts.

Among those thoughts was this one: Today is Tyler's birthday.

Back home, we ordered pizza. Tyler, the youngest of our four birth children, half-heartedly blew out thirty-three candles atop a store-bought cake and absorbed the burden of loss his birthdays would now carry. Still, I glimpsed a gift of God's provision in this cross my son would bear. I remembered his birth as Tyler, a delightful "surprise" baby who had arrived several days late, extinguished the candles. He had become a certified financial planner, the one to whom Ray had entrusted my fiscal future. I prayed Tyler could someday receive the gift of this shared date and release the burden of it.

"Hey guys, let's circle up," I suggested after dinner, a family tradition that corralled and quieted our large numbers. We circled up to pray before family meals at birthday and holiday gatherings. In a few days, we would circle up around Ray's grave in Colorado as Nick lowered his father's cremated remains into the ground. But that night we rearranged living room chairs into a circle to plan Ray's celebration of life service.

In the days to follow, while we were still in North Carolina, Kristi marshaled the troops to get me unpacked, then stayed up late into the night, visiting with my children long after I had gone to bed. Chad tamed the lawn, Nick oversaw construction and picture-hanging projects, and Brooke and Tyler helped me make decisions at the mortuary. Others bought groceries, prepared food, or ran errands. Everybody picked up a piece of our shared universe, making it lighter for all.

We circled up in the evenings before it was time to return to Colorado, honing Ray's service into the tribute we wanted to offer him. In the end, it held fragments from all of us—a mosaic of our story of chipped and imperfect lives made beautiful by the love we shared for the rock of our family. From the distance of years, what I treasure most was the give-and-take process with every voice being heard. It was a taste of how we would learn to do life together without him. In circling up, in telling the story, our collective healing had begun.

If Ray were here, he would have tears in his voice.

Quiet Reflections

- Tell your story below, one more time.

- Even with a terminal diagnosis and time to prepare, we are seldom ready for the death of those we love. How were you supported in the early hours and days after your loss? What would have been more helpful? What would you tell those who might now be in your situation?

- Where did you see God's grace in your loved one's homegoing? Or did you? Write your prayer of thanks or a prayer of lament.

Chapter 10

Blessing of the Birds

He will cover you with his feathers,
and under his wings you will find refuge;
his faithfulness will be your shield and rampart.
Psalm 91:4

September 20, 2015, Colorado

"Good morning," I said to my daughter-in-law as I slipped into her kitchen. "You're up early. How did you sleep?"

"Okay, I guess. And you?"

"Pretty well," I said as I poured myself a cup of coffee and remembered all we had shared the previous day. "I'll be back in a little while," I said, scooping up keys from the counter and heading toward the door. "I think I'll have my morning coffee with Ray."

We had attended Ray's celebration of life service the previous morning, our tribute born from the circling-up evenings in North Carolina. Like others around me, I rose to leave at the conclusion of the service when ushers stood beside our pew to dismiss the family. Then, almost as an afterthought, I glanced at the large portrait of Ray resting on an easel at the front of the church before I turned to walk up the aisle. And I swear I saw him wink at me.

Maybe I *could* survive.

Our family gathered later that afternoon for a private graveside ceremony. Sunshine and warmth had invited us to linger— with each other and our own thoughts. Then, slowly, the gathered dispersed until it was time for me to leave too. But driving away from the cemetery, I vowed to return this morning.

My children and I chose to bury Ray's ashes in a rural cemetery with a view of the Colorado valley we love and have called home for nearly thirty years. Arriving there again, that Colorado morning was typical—sunny, still, and magnificent.

I had driven past this historic churchyard cemetery thousands of times in the busyness of our comings and goings. I'd been charmed by the quintessential chapel nestled beyond the gates that offered comfort and a grandparent's wisdom to those within its shadow. That morning it wasn't just a historic, charming landmark anymore. It held a piece of real estate that anchored my story.

Slowing, I neared the cemetery entrance, feeling the crunch of gravel beneath my tires as I turned from the two-lane highway onto a narrow, rocky lane leading to Ray's grave. Tears erupted when I spotted yesterday's flowers standing guard over clumps of earth holding the remains of the man I loved, strong arms that had wrapped me in bear hugs and soft eyes that had whispered, "I love you."

I parked the car and sat motionless. I had no script for what should come next. Gripping my travel mug filled with lukewarm coffee, I opened the door, slid from behind the wheel, and walked slowly to his grave. "Baby, I'm here," I whispered, bewildered, searching for something I couldn't name.

After forty-two years of marriage, we knew each other better than we knew ourselves; we could finish each other's sentences without a second guess. Ray and I had prepared ourselves for his death, and my widowhood, as best we could. We had said things we needed to say, forgiven each other, and shared heart-to-heart talks about death, dying, and the legacy he wanted to leave. And I held him, weeping, as he took his last labored breath.

Funeral memories and wilted flowers screamed "Widow!" as I stood at Ray's grave that day. I had feared this loss with a dread that erased all else but grief. I had never considered how the presence of God, the tenderness of Jesus, or the strength of the Holy Spirit might comfort and strengthen me, yet new thoughts and heart murmurings had begun to stir. God's grace softening the blow of this loss had been real and profound in numerous ways over the past few days.

What if my fear of suffering turned out to be worse than the suffering itself?

Oh Lord, I really don't know how to pray right now. But I do know that I'm scared and sad and overwhelmed. I need something more—just for me. I need something with your fingerprints all over it to let me know you see me and are with me.

Aimlessly I returned to my car, slipped behind the wheel, sipped my coffee, and waited. For what?

Then I noticed birds. Scores of them flocked around Ray's grave. They flitted from branch to branch and chirped bossily to one another while hopping on his grave or circling above it. What a party they hosted! Oh, how he would have loved it.

Ray enjoyed birds. He would pause to watch them, putz with his feeders, and patiently help the grandkids fill the feeders in our wooded yard. I loved that about him. But birds were his thing. I'd never really taken an interest in them until they had quietly morphed into part of our retirement plan.

One evening before his diagnosis, we were talking about our approaching empty nest and impending retirements. "I'm concerned about our expectations of each other when we retire," I said. "I don't think I want to do it the way you do."

We had watched other couples stumble in this season. Some drifted apart from each other, while others became suffocating and inseparable. How could we navigate this transition and do it well? Over time we agreed we could each be boss of ourselves. We would develop our individual interests and cultivate mutual ones.

"So, what else could we do together besides golf?" I asked. I knew there would be no more business functions, projects, or travel to share, and no more children's school activities or sporting events to attend—the essence of what had dominated our calendars for decades.

"Well, I do really like birds," he said.

"I can do that!" I quipped. "Plus, I love how you take time to be still and notice them. I want to learn how to do that too."

So I did.

I began to learn the names and characteristics of common birds visiting our feeders. Together we identified shorebirds when we traveled to the coast. I became awed by their beauty and God's creative expression in each of them.

That morning at Ray's grave, I noted scores of plain brown sparrows mingled with stunning mountain bluebirds as they darted about, enlivening the branches of nearby trees while outlying pines remained still and empty. I watched and listened, mesmerized by their sheer numbers. Then, startled, I ducked as a lone bluebird dive-bombed straight toward me, veering sharply upward before smashing into my windshield. I gasped. Within a few seconds, it happened again. And then a third time, as if the birds, under someone's command, lined up, took aim, and targeted me behind the driver's wheel.

My peaceful cup of coffee was long forgotten as I murmured, "I get it, Lord."

Punctuating the obvious, a bluebird fluttered outside the passenger window as if waving to get my attention, then perched atop my side mirror. Stealing sideways glances through soft brown eyes, he seemed to be asking "Are you watching this?"

My heart raced. The three diving bluebirds that had startled me to attention, and the beauty and nearness of the one perched within my grasp, captivated me. My prayer had been answered.

That morning I had come to the cemetery to share a cup of coffee with my beloved and to ask God to show me he would be with me on this widow's journey. He did. He sent birds. God's grace had trumped my fear. He took a theme from our love story, fused it with a metaphor from Psalm 91:4, "He will cover you with his feathers, and under his wings you will find refuge," and displayed an answer to my prayer when I needed it most.

I left the cemetery that morning assured that God was with me, that he was enough for today, and that he was in my tomorrows and would gently lead me there. This was a "knowing" that nestled in, bore down, and intended to take up residence deep within my soul.

God's tender display of love hugged my heart, a gift to keep in this season of letting go.

Quiet Reflections

- Where have you found refuge in your sorrow? Has it been life giving or life numbing? What would it mean for you to find refuge under God's wings?

- Consider God's grace. When has it been real and profound? How did it trump fear . . . or did it?

- In Mark 10:46–51, Jesus encountered Bartimaeus, a blind beggar along the side of the road, as he and his disciples were leaving Jericho. When Bartimaeus heard that Jesus was passing by, he cried out, "Jesus, Son of David, have mercy on me!" Jesus called the blind man to him and said, "What do you want me to do for you?" "Rabbi, I want to see," said Bartimaeus. Jesus sees us in our pain. He hears us, even in a crowd. And he asks us the same question: "What do you want me to do for you?" How would you answer him?

Part Three

Into the Deep

I will go before you and will level the mountains; I
will break down gates of bronze
and cut through bars of iron.
I will give you hidden treasures,
riches stored in secret places,
so that you may know that I am the Lord,
the God of Israel, who summons you by name.
Isaiah 45:2–3

Solitude

Solitude is the furnace of transformation.
—Henry Nouwen, *The Way of the Heart*

*When I am in solitude, the presence of God is so
real and so full that there is nothing else I want.*
—Ruth Haley Barton, *Sacred Rhythms*

"Mom, I can't go back to school now," Abby said shortly after Ray's funeral while we were still in Colorado. "Can I go to North Carolina with you? I feel close to Dad at the beach. I really need that right now. And honestly, I don't even know if I ever want to go back to school."

"Of course, you can—for as long as you need," I said, wondering how this would work. I had no idea what to expect in the unprecedented terrain of my own grief. Could I forestall its impact to help my daughter navigate hers?

Abby, the youngest of our seven children, was three weeks into her junior year of college in Oregon when Ray died. Adopted from India at sixteen months old, she had already lost one set of parents whom she had yet to grieve. My beautiful, pragmatic daughter wore a "no trespassing" sign on her heart. But death violated her boundary, and grief ravaged her soul.

Together we returned to North Carolina two days after Ray's funeral. In the days to follow, Abby and I found solace in walking on the beach together—sometimes in silence, other times sharing our thoughts. We felt close to Ray there. But something more drew us, compelled us to walk barefoot on that intersect of sand and water where fragments of spent waves stretched to tickle our toes before tumbling over themselves in retreat, then paused, preparing to do it all over again. The majestic roar of the deep seeped into grieving souls, leaving behind a remnant of its strength to sustain us, a reminder that earth is not our home.

The Spirit who has hovered over the waters since the third day of creation seemed to ride those spent waves beachward and occupy that intersected space—space that mirrored the mystery of life and death, the thinness of the veil between the two, and their connectedness. We sensed God, in whose presence Ray now lived, walking with us on that beach. We needed that connection.

In our cocoon-like days, we sat by the fire, ate popcorn for dinner, sipped cocoa from matching cups, and let days melt one into another until it was time.

"I think I'm ready to go back," Abby said eight days later. And she did.

I busied myself the following week, determined to render this house a home before Colorado friends arrived for the visit we had planned as couples before Ray and I left Colorado. *I wonder if they'll still come,* I remember thinking at Ray's funeral. Of course, I knew they would.

"I'm going to walk this journey with you," Ruth assured me shortly before Ray and I moved. We had become friends as young mothers. We babysat each other's children, rooted for each other in our diverse careers, and grew close through similar faith journeys. She would be a lifeline in deep waters. I was thankful she and her husband, Rick, were coming. And that I had things to do to prepare for their arrival.

Despite the progress Kristi and my children had made, moving boxes still littered the garage and mocked me from every room. I tackled them one by one. For the first time in my life, decisions about where things would go were mine alone. I filled cupboards, made beds, hung towels, and arranged outdoor furniture—until pictures captured my attention.

"All Because Two People Fell in Love" shouted the large, rectangular plaque under which eight family photos begged to be hung: Ray and me at the beach and each of our seven children with their families. These people were as vital to life as my next breath.

But hanging pictures, like grilling and finances, had been Ray's job. I rummaged through a toolbox in the garage to find a hammer. *Measure twice, cut once,* niggled a carpentry proverb as I retraced my steps back into the house clutching the hammer and a fist full of nails. About hanging things, I wondered, is it *measure twice, hammer once?* If I cover up errant nail holes with a picture, I reasoned, what difference does it make?

By evening's end, one plaque and eight pictures hung neatly in formation. Obedient soldiers saluting my "there's-usually-more-than-one-right-answer" philosophy—if you didn't count the nail holes that didn't show.

It was starting to feel like home.

October 8–10, 2015

"I can't believe you're actually here!" I said a few days later as I hugged Ruth and Rick at the front door and accepted the beautiful flowers they brought. We chatted about their trip, the blessing of the nearby beach, and how good it felt to be together as I showed them to their upstairs room. "Why don't you take some time to unpack and get settled a bit," I suggested. "Then we'll grab some chairs and head for the beach."

Over the next two days, we strolled and sat on the beach, ate dinner at Daddy Mac's, and stayed up late talking. Pleasant conversation and comfortable silence filled our days, making it easy to pretend Ray had stepped from the room but would be right back. Though their presence eased the pain of loss, this visit, born of friendship that had ebbed and flowed through three decades, would be the gracious on-ramp into a set-apart season that awaited their goodbye.

Since my return to North Carolina three weeks earlier, I had treasured time with Abby, unpacked and resettled my home, and cherished this visit with Ruth. I worked hard to be present. To stay positive. To delay the impact of grief until I could be alone.

Standing on my front porch at the end of their stay, I watched them back from the driveway onto the quiet street in front of my home. They waved, smiled, and slowly drove off. I waved back until they rounded the corner at the end of the block three houses away. I hoped they couldn't see my tears. Sobbing, I opened the front door and felt myself shrink from the inside out like a deflating party balloon.

What now? What do I do with the empty days and endless nights that stretched before me? What rhythms do I keep? And which ones, like dead autumn leaves, dangling with no purpose until whisked by a gust of wind to gather in a heap of lifeless litter, do I let go? No husband. No children at home. No job. No schedule, demands, or responsibilities. What will fill the silence and satisfy my soul in the absence of what gave my life meaning?

Walking into my silent home, I faced the reality of a life I didn't want—widowhood. An uncertain future of solitary days. No more distractions. No more family and friends for the foreseeable future. No script. And no plan for the white space that filled my calendar or the empty space inside of me.

No more Ray. He hadn't just stepped from the room for a moment. My last reason to say his name out loud so I could hear it, pretend I was still a wife, half of a couple had vanished with my friends' departure.

How do I learn to be me without you?

Turning back was not an option. There weren't enough pieces left to reassemble my old life. Here among strangers for a set-apart time, I would heal and prepare to reenter life in some repurposed version of me, but I could never be the same.

Life as I knew it had shattered and fallen from my bones. I would have to grow a new one, piece by piece, like working a jigsaw puzzle without a picture on the box to show me what it's supposed to look like. Sensing I needed to be alone and invisible, I closed the door behind me and crossed the threshold into solitude.

As days slid one into another, I nestled deep within solitude's womb. Gently held within this private place and tethered to the Source of life, I received the nourishment I needed to survive. I walked by the ocean, read Scripture and good books, lingered over coffee with Jesus, journaled to wrestle down fear, and grieved well. In this still, dark place, I heard echoes of my heavenly Father's heartbeat within the rhythm of my own broken yet thumping heart.

Henri Nouwen describes solitude as "the place of the great struggle and the great encounter—the struggle against the compulsions of the false self, and the encounter with the loving God who offers himself as the substance of the new self . . . it is the place of conversion, the place where the old self dies and the new self is born, the place where the emergence of the new man and the new woman occurs."[10]

I nurtured my umbilical connection as days unfolded into

weeks, then months. Although I had professed a faith in Christ since I was seventeen, there was a kind of being born again happening in me as God's presence infused this sacred space.

Static cleared. The thrumming cacophony from decades of busyness ceased. Brain fog lifted, slowly evaporating until one day I realized it was gone. I asked some voices from my past to leave. My tolerance for random noise had diminished, and I could no longer abide the adrenaline or unhealthy chatter it produced.

My soul yearned for solitude like plants that reach toward sunshine; I, the created, longed for my Creator. Having grown deficient, I required large infusions to heal and to surrender the future I had wanted so I could receive the one God had for me. I was alone but not lonely during this rich time. It allowed me to both grieve my losses and nurture a flickering hope.

I gravitated toward peace and quiet. My external world shifted to mirror my internal one as I gently picked up the pieces of my life I wanted to keep and rearranged them in ways that suited me. I met a neighbor while walking and accepted her invitation to join a weekly Bible study that met in her home. I became friends with another adoptive mom, both of us northern transplants who shared the language of adoption realities. I said yes to movie and lunch invitations when I wanted to and no when I did not. It was a quiet spirit, born of solitude, that allowed me to appreciate those new friends and experiences that nourished and healed me as I continued to engage with grief, loss, and letting go. I learned joy can occupy the same space as sorrow.

Solitude had found me. It became the container in which I immersed myself and from which I drank. There I encountered the gentleness and kindness of Jesus and found the courage to take the next step.

Quiet Reflections

- What do you think is the difference between being alone and solitude?

- What nourishes your soul? Are you getting your minimum daily requirement? What changes would you like to make to strengthen your spiritual health?

- What voices from your past do you want to ask to leave? Write your letter of termination to their power over your life here.

Chapter 12

Follow Me

Get away with me and you'll recover your life . . .
Walk with me and work with me—watch how I
do it. Learn the unforced rhythms of grace.
Matthew 11:28–29 MSG

October 21, 2015

I filled a small thermos with two cups of morning coffee and grabbed my beach chair, journal, devotional, and pen. Tossing them in the car, I backed out of the garage for the six-minute drive-through beachside neighborhoods and tourist shops, and across the bridge to Topsail Island. A few blocks later, I pulled into the parking lot. Warm wind whipped my hair as I shed flip-flops and pitched them into the car. Gathering my gear, I gingerly stepped onto coarse gravel.

Hidden behind the dune, the sea thundered, its sound filling this space with majesty. My heart quickened as to the intimate sound of a lover's voice, a caress, or soft eyes. If my heart had arms, they would have been reaching, stretching, begging to be held and comforted. I hurried to the beach-access ramp and stepped onto weathered planks, smooth and warm. They carried me over the dune and into the feast. Having tasted and been satisfied, I had come yet again. Expectant.

Cresting the dune, I stopped. This ocean beauty never failed to take my breath away—a palette of blues and grays tumbling to rearrange itself and melting into the horizon while reflecting the sky's changing mood. Here Deep speaks to deep and the Creator to the created. My sad but healing heart heard the Comforter's voice. It calmed me, untangled the cords that bound grief, and offered new perspective.

The moon's gravitational pull had drained the ocean to low tide, making long my walk to the lapping waves on a nearly deserted beach. I unfolded my chair and eased into its low-slung embrace. Grateful for the gentle breeze that tempered the sun's heat on that cloudless morning, I savored unhurried time and allowed the surf's ceaseless rumble to unravel emotional knots as God's voice murmured, coaxed, and healed me.

I took a slow pull of coffee. Opening my devotional, these words from the gospel of Matthew touched a tender place in me: "Get away with me and you'll recover your life . . . Walk with me and work with me—watch how I do it. Learn the unforced rhythms of grace" (Matthew 11:28–29 MSG).

As I sat on a beach halfway across the country from home, family, and friends, life resembled almost nothing of what I had known just two months ago. Some days I felt lost, fragmented, and maybe even guilty that I was alive but Ray wasn't. If given the choice, however, I knew he would not return; this comforted me. He was home, free of the tensions of living in this in-between space, and of his disease. That morning I began to pick up the corner of the universe containing our story, knowing it was mine to figure out, as I watched a seagull soar on invisible currents—flying solo.

"I want to recover your life." Pondering these words that came to mind as the bird glided effortlessly above the water, I asked, "Is this from you, Jesus?"

Just then, a small gray-and-white feather fluttered beside me and rested at the foot of my chair. I watched intrigued as another wisp of air lifted and carried it a few feet down the beach, where again it landed on wet sand. It playfully beckoned. I stood to follow the feather down the beach as it toppled ahead, born by the rhythm of the breeze—lifting with each flurry, then floating to the ground when creation inhaled.

"Follow me."

So I did. Until finally I reached to pick it up. Smiling, I walked back to my chair and tucked the feather between pages of my devotional, certain it was part of my story. I remembered the blessing of the birds at the cemetery, and now, a timely feather reminded me again of God's presence and invited me to follow him, even in my grief.

As I sat on the beach that morning, six weeks after Ray had died, I took stock of where I was. I felt awakened to changes, inside and out—golden-brown skin and sun-kissed cheeks, a reflection of my beach-going life, and a heart growing calm, more open, and wider as grief bowed to gratitude. I became aware of God's presence in and around me at the ocean like nowhere else. A hunger was being satisfied. I had found manna in the wilderness of widowhood.

I knew I needed to remember that day for the landlocked season ahead and store the memories and insights as food for soul-hungry days. I lingered, face lifted skyward, willing this memory to sear itself into mind and heart: the smell of salt-laden breeze tousling age-whitened hair, warm sun that bathed forsaken skin, a bird flying solo, and the relentless song of the ocean.

"I want to recover your life."

By then I believed I would survive the grief of Ray's death, but this invitation was for more. It was one that would help me make sense of our story, recover my life without Ray, and teach me to fly solo. Hope seeped in, living water for parched places, making soft the ground. Mystery awakened hunger. But at that moment, I was content to wait and watch.

Shortly after Ray died, I gave myself the gift of an unlimited book budget. I immersed myself in the stories and language of others who had survived loss and allowed God to transform them through suffering. I read books written by professionals who had studied and written about grief, loss, and faith. I had minimized and moved on when I got hurt. Learning a better way, I was determined to lean into this pain for as long as it took to heal.

I embraced silence and solitude in the weeks and months that followed and reflected on Scripture and the wisdom of others. Almost unnoticed, the posture and orientation of my heart had slowly begun to shift; I grew more attentive to the gentle movement of the Spirit in my life. Words became few. I listened. And I noticed how God communicated with me.

"Clear communication can be very difficult between people, even with the advantage of inflection, expression, and gesture," writes Marjorie Thompson in her book *Soul Feast: An Invitation to the Christian Spiritual Life.* "How much more confusing it is to communicate with One who is invisible, intangible, inaudible, and inscrutable! Yet God desires to be known and has many ways of communicating with us if we are willing to listen."[11]

Thompson goes on to say that Scripture, creation, other people, circumstances, dreams, journal keeping, symbols and images, and subtle and mysterious things like intuition, conviction and the feeling that something is "meant to be" are all ways that God speaks to us. [12]

That morning as I crested the dune, read the verses in Matthew that touched my heart, and followed the feather down the beach, God was communicating with me through creation, Scripture, and symbols. And I was listening.

Charles Stanley, in *How to Listen to God,* says: "Whatever our situation may call for—guidance, comfort, assurance, strength, perseverance, faith, joy, peace—God's voice will supply. The answer will not be found in the noise and rumble (earthquake, wind, and fire) of the world or religion. It is seldom that we will hear accurately from God in the rush of traffic, the din of the office, or the clatter of friends. God wishes to speak to us individually, and for that we must be committed to seek solitude, however brief."[13]

These teachings validated what I had begun to experience in my times of solitude. God was showing me in numerous ways that yes, he was present and I was not forgotten—and now, his whisper to *"Follow me . . . I want to recover your life."*

Opening my devotional, I picked up the feather nestled within the pages—my invitation to follow Jesus on a further journey.

I said yes. Then discovered it had already begun.

Quiet Reflections

- Where do you feel close to God? What makes you aware of God's presence in and around you?

- What does it mean to you to listen to God? Look back at Marjorie Thompson's list of some of the ways God speaks to us. How does he generally speak to you?

- "Get away with me and you'll recover your life . . . Walk with me and work with me—watch how I do it. Learn the unforced rhythms of grace" (Matthew 11:28–29 MSG). Read these words again, slowly. Underline the word or phrase that stands out to you. Consider it within the context of your life. If you sense an invitation, what is it?

Rhythms of Grace

*The language of rhythms speaks of ebb and flow,
creativity and beauty, music and dancing, joy and
giving ourselves over to a force or a power that is
beyond ourselves and is deeply good. Over time, as
we surrender ourselves to new life rhythms, they
help us to surrender old behaviors, attitudes and
practices so that we can be shaped by new ones.*
—Ruth Haley Barton, *Sacred Rhythms*

Fall 2015–Spring 2016, North Carolina

As a rule, I don't make important decisions before I'm fully
awake and have had my coffee. They usually don't turn out
well. But lying in bed one morning a few days after Ray died, I
established the trajectory of my healing when I made the first
conscious decision about my future. It didn't come from courage,
wisdom, bravery, or faith. It originated from a practical view of
my circumstances: I woke up that morning and was still alive,
unsure if that was good news or bad news. My thoughts flashed
both backward and forward—backward to health issues that had
plagued my ancestors and forward to my future that might in-

clude them. Since I lived alone, no one would care or even know what lifestyle choices I made or how they might affect me. My health and well-being were my responsibility.

Although the Lord has numbered my days, I could influence the quality of them. Therefore, before I flung the covers aside and stepped into a new day, I decided I had better take care of myself, just in case I was going to keep waking up each morning. It proved to be a good decision. One that opened the door for rhythms of grace to find me.

I started with eating well. That meant taking time to plan, shop, prepare healthy foods, and limit those that were not. I faltered along the way when convenience and overpowering desire for comfort food hijacked my good intentions. Yet overall, the process of nourishing my body felt like a tending and caring rhythm inherent in creation. Genesis 1:14 tells us that God made the sun, moon, and stars to "serve as signs to mark sacred times, and days and years." And later, after God created Adam, he put him in the Garden of Eden "to work it and take care of it" (Genesis 2:15).

Grief is sacred time. And mine beckoned stillness—like a field lying fallow, unplanted and bare for a season of rest. I needed to honor that tending and caring desire of my createdness.

I pictured a still, barren tree whose roots dug deep in search of water and nutrients to sustain it until its season for new growth, flourishing leaves, and fruitful harvest would emerge. The rhythm of seasons was as certain for me as it was for that tree. My barren season would both nourish me and pass, but it could not be rushed.

Alan Fadling, in his book *An Unhurried Life: Following Jesus' Rhythms of Work and Rest,* describes Jesus as "an unhurried Savior."[14] One from whom we can learn "to move at the pace of grace."[15] For a while, my pace of grace was stillness, which slowly birthed a deeper sense of order and unhurried faithfulness in the rhythms of God.

Like the rhythm of grace that pulled me into its orbit each morning.

Walking into the kitchen, I'd open the slender cabinet above the stove, reach for a coffee filter, pat it into place, add two scoops of grounds, fill the water receptacle, tap the lid closed, and press Start. Then I'd busy myself until the lifeblood of my morning dripped into the waiting carafe, filling my kitchen with gurgling sounds and the rich aroma of coffee. After pouring a steaming cup and adding creamer until clouds appeared, I settled into my chair, ready to visit and pray—like mornings when Ray and I shared our coffee time, two cups each.

Such ordinary rhythms that once sustained me began to atrophy and die when Ray did. Our marriage rhythms no longer fit. I let them go and refused to thoughtlessly replace them, choosing instead to live each day as a one-of-a-kind event. I ate when I felt hungry and slept when I got tired. I read books, took naps, walked on the beach, and went to movies by myself. I didn't set an alarm. Occasionally I had popcorn and wine for dinner. I watched golf tournaments on Sunday afternoons, made friends at church and in my neighborhood, and walked the dogs. I liked solitude and silence. And I waited in their company for new rhythms—ones that suited my reshaped life: widowhood, early retirement, and an empty nest.

I got to decide how to spend my time. No longer driven by the needs and schedules of others, I noticed what I wanted and needed. As I respected my needs and wishes, rhythms emerged. Some were new, others merely tweaked.

Like morning coffee. Now *I* make it, instead of Ray, and still drink two cups. Jesus, rather than my husband, has become my morning companion. As with Ray, I talk *and* listen. Lingering lends itself to that. So does intimacy. In this familiar rhythm, I discovered holy and tailor-made alterations for my reshaped life—deeper rhythms of rest, prayer with fewer words, and greater hope that Jesus's presence will fill the broken places Ray's death created. "Satisfy me in the morning with your unfailing love," based on Psalm 90:14, became the cry of my heart when I found him waiting each morning.

Since the day I pursued the feather down the beach, heard the invitation to *Follow me . . . I want to recover your life,* and read in my devotional, "Get away with me and you'll recover your life . . . Walk with me and work with me—watch how I do it. Learn the unforced rhythms of grace" (Matthew 11:28–30 MSG), I had been captivated by Jesus's words. I longed to be bathed in quietness and peace. I also clung to a delicious absence of shoulds and how-tos.

Unforced rhythms of grace became a way of seeing and being in time: unhurried, present, and trusting. They led to a spiritual posture of following, not controlling; responding, not initiating; nurturing my inner life, not distracting it. I *could* live peaceably within the constraints of my createdness without trying to overcome or improve them—respecting the fearfully and wonderfully made parts that need to sleep, rest, eat, pray, create, and grieve.

I worked a little bit each day in the weeks after Ray's death to unpack the remaining moving boxes. This grounded me. The diminishing number of boxes marked tangible progress on an intangible journey.

The last boxes lining my office wall were filled with Ray's files: tax returns, insurance policies and investment information, business and property files, birth certificates, passports and Social Security documents, banking, and billing statements. It took six weeks to unpack, sort, read, understand, shred, or organize these records into a system that worked for me. I studied the notes I had written on those Saturday mornings Ray and I sat around the dining room table when he tutored me for this task. I would figure it out. In those early days, I started with monthly bills.

Paying bills began as a spontaneous sort of thing—one that demanded my attention but had no rhythm in my life beyond my capacity to live with unfinished business. I had no experience to help me know how to schedule this job or to muster the emotional capacity to even want to. These would come later. I did, however, find the early stage of this process predictable.

When unfinished business called my name, I shoved distractions aside and trusted the process. I slipped the checkbook, calculator, and stamps from their drawer, pulled up newly created spreadsheets on my computer that I had made to track these monthly expenses, and tackled the stack of bills on my desk. I wrote and signed each check, placed it in the envelope I'd prepared, and sealed it. Then I scribbled the date and my initials on the invoice, a left-over habit from work when I approved agency expenditures. Once I had slogged my way to the bottom of the pile, I scooped up the envelopes, walked them to the mailbox at the end of my driveway, then checked "pay bills" off my to-do list. Everything neat and tidy—until the next batch would clutter my desk and exceed my capacity to live with unfinished business.

After forty-two years, three months, and ten days of Ray paying the bills, it was my job now.

We didn't talk much in the hours before he died. An oxygen mask and comfort meds hindered him; grief silenced me. Despite the heartbreak of his terminal diagnosis, it had given us time to prepare me for this chore. Yet in Ray's final hours when words felt burdensome and inadequate during the hard work of dying and letting go, he did ask for paper and pencil. Slowly he scrawled bank account information and noted our credit card payment was due the next day.

What? But I knew it wasn't about banking or a credit card bill. It was about love, about doing the only thing left that he could do for his hasn't-balanced-a-checkbook-since-college wife. "Sweetheart, you don't have to worry about this now," I said, gently slipping the pencil and tiny notebook from his hands. "I'll figure it out."

And I have. Oh, how I long to show him spreadsheets and systems I've created, and online banking skills I've learned to do what he did with a legal pad, chicken scratch, and an Albert Einstein mess of a desk that drove me nuts. I'm doing it my way, managing this bill-paying journey with no end when it calls my name.

Over time I recognized a rhythm of grief reflected in my bill-paying ritual—a hit-or-miss sort of thing that defied scheduling but demanded my attention. When unfinished business whispered my name, I shoved distractions aside and cried, until I was done.

Figuring out how to manage Ray's other responsibilities took time. First, I shed the notion that I had to do them all. Then I clarified my options. I saw four: (1) do it, (2) learn how to do it and then do it, (3) hire someone to do it, or (4) let it go.

About mowing the lawn, I chose option one: do it.

I grew up mowing the lawn and farm pastures around our country home. I like working outside, and Ray and I had enjoyed doing yard work together. But when a hedge trimmer slashed my hand (user error!) when I was pregnant and I ended up in the ER for stitches, power tools became off limits. I dug in the dirt and planted flowers after that. Kids also helped as they matured. Three sturdy boys did most of the mowing until each left home. But Ray couldn't mow the lawn in North Carolina.

No problem. Smaller yard and no hedges. I've got this. We bought a lawnmower shortly after we arrived in August. Some assembly required. So Ray put it together sitting on a lawn chair in the backyard. I mowed that day and continued to mow the yard every week for two months after Ray died. "This started out to be an outdoor day," I wrote in my journal one November evening, "until I broke the lawnmower running over the water meter."

I abandoned option one and opted for a hybrid of options three and four for this lawnmowing chore: hire it out and let it go. A reasonably priced lawn service agreed to pick up the slack, every Tuesday morning, just like clockwork.

Sometimes rhythms of grace have more than one right answer.

I removed "should" from my vocabulary and guarded white space on my calendar when I began to reengage with life. Unsure of when unfinished grief would whisper my name, I lived within the boundaries of my emotional bandwidth: whatever I did needed to nurture me. Ongoing commitments made me hyperventilate and didn't make the cut.

I began by writing letters and sending cards and small gifts to family and friends. One evening I attended a neighborhood women's Bible study; it required only a pleasant smile. Then I tried a yoga class at the community center. One winter morning I stopped by my favorite gift shop on the island; it was off season, and I was the only customer in the store. The owner greeted me, and we chatted. I said I was looking for a centerpiece for my dining room table, something "beachy." I didn't have anything like that, coming from Colorado. I listened to her story of loss and shared mine. I left an hour later with no centerpiece but a part-time job. It provided the beginning of structure.

I met wonderful people, locals and tourists, while I worked there and learned about this island I had grown to love. I visited kids and grandkids in Oregon, Missouri, and Colorado, surprised by the grief I felt in being with them without Ray. Eventually I enrolled in an evening writing class, taught by a local author at the junior college near my home.

Rhythms of grace found me in each endeavor as I practiced doing life alone.

Sometimes rhythms of grace found me. Other times I needed to move forward in faith to claim them.

I noticed other widows in my neighborhood and church community and asked if they'd like to get together. They said they would, and our Flying Solo group began meeting monthly. Some, like me, were newly widowed, while others were more seasoned. Although each woman experienced her unique story, we shared much in common. I gleaned insights from them that helped me see beyond the ragged pain and form realistic expectations for my solitary future. My story wasn't the center of anyone's universe; I was the one tasked with living it. Still, it felt good to know I wasn't alone.

There is a rhythm of grace in shared grief—empathy, compassion, and unhurried helping—as we slow our pace to match another's and help share their burden by our presence.

"Such intertwining of death and life, sorrow and rejoicing, is always part of the Christian message," says Emilie Griffin in *Small Surrenders*. "Ours is a religion of heartbreak and celebration, a message of God's deep love for his wounded world."[16]

This is where I found myself in the early months after Ray died—integrating the grief of his death with hope for the future, letting old rhythms go and establishing new ones. Hope did not negate grief: hope agreed with God that he had left me here for a purpose, that he is in my tomorrows, and that he will gently lead me there.

Learning to live in response to the rhythms of God's heart was changing me. Yet unsettledness lurked, preparing to throw a fit in the cavern of untamed time.

Quiet Reflections

- How has loss led to surrendering yourself to new life rhythms? Or has it? What behaviors, attitudes, and practices have you let go of? What holy alterations, tailor-made for you, have you found in existing rhythms? What new rhythms of grace have found you?

- Learning to manage the responsibilities your spouse used to do can be a significant learning curve in the face of loss. What have you had to do, learn to do, hire out, or let go of? Name one thing and describe the process and how you felt about it.

- Learning rhythms of grace applies to how we think about and treat ourselves. How are you doing with honoring your fearfully and wonderfully made parts that need to sleep, rest, eat, pray, create, and grieve? Is there anything you need to seek help with? Write your prayer to God.

Unsettled

When suffering shatters the carefully kept vase that is our lives, God stoops to pick up the pieces. But he doesn't put them back together as a restoration project patterned after our former selves. Instead, he sifts through the rubble and selects some of the shards as raw material for another project—a mosaic that tells the story of redemption.
—Ken Gire, *The North Face of God*

December 2015

I had entered a season of unsettledness, of being out of sync with myself. Time didn't fit anymore. I thought I knew how to manage it and produce within it, but time had morphed into a foreign language I was trying to understand.

The dictionary defines unsettled as: "Not in a state of order or calmness; disturbed; likely to change or vary; not determined or resolved; uncertain or doubtful."[17] Though accurate, these definitions were incomplete.

My unsettledness included an element of darkness—not scary dark, but a hidden darkness that nurtures growth, rich soil sheltering spring seeds. I was listening for a whisper to show me the way and waiting in an in-between time that struggles to balance the shift from "what was" to "what will come." That unsettledness rose from living in the rubble of my former life.

Even my body was unsettled and likely to change. I suffered from the lingering effects of pneumonia for most of December. Hip pain drove me to an orthopedic surgeon who confirmed a joint replacement was inevitable. While not surprised by this news, I felt like I'd been struck by a torpedo. I had cared for my mother following her hip replacement surgery several years earlier despite my bent toward squeamishness. Seeing people in pain made me want to cry or run away and hide. I hoped I would never have to endure what she did. I was afraid. My greatest concern, however, was having to go through this surgery and recovery without Ray's support.

My body had kept score of my losses, then shouted its rebellion. It had betrayed me. I could no longer take good health for granted.

I missed the predictability of living on autopilot yet appreciated my freedom and heightened awareness. Sometimes I felt afraid of this unfamiliar way of living. Was this unsettledness detrimental or essential for my healing? Hard to tell. Like tender shoots popping up in the garden after spring rains, distinguishing weeds from flowers can take a while.

Additionally, unsettledness had also sprouted in once-occupied space. The administration of dying—dealing with death-related paperwork, phone calls, thank-you notes, estate and investment issues, insurance claims, and medical bills—had begun to subside. When these duties that had lent temporary structure and purpose to my life began to go away, untamed time replaced them. Yet I continued to resist stuffing days with distractions.

As a recovering type A, I slowly replaced obsolete paradigms with ones that fit. Allowing God to recover my life, I followed him into my sadness and received comfort. I remained still. I craved feeling loved again and wanted to experience the intimacy of God's presence. For brief times, in that space, the ache of Ray's absence was relieved. Lacking desire or the energy to hurry, and with nowhere else to go, I lingered.

I began to trust this unhurried posture—waiting to let life and healing unfold. I savored such an unfolding over Thanksgiving, our first holiday without Ray.

Conflicting feelings followed me and my family to Colorado when we gathered to share this milestone. Dreading the unknown, I wanted this holiday to just be over, yet I was looking forward to being together. Although Ray's absence was palpable, so was his presence as we recounted old memories and made new ones.

"Remember the good," Ray had asked of us shortly before he died.

So we did. Tears, laughter, and heartwarming diversions from "the littles" flowed organically throughout our four-day visit. Joy cushioned sorrow's sharp edges. Our time was tender and good, although my mother's sporadic presence at our gatherings and her failing health reminded us again of life's uncertainty.

Emboldened by our successful Thanksgiving, I began to prepare for Christmas when I returned to North Carolina. I bought a tree, pulled the unwieldy box from the back of my SUV, and dragged it into the house. Plying open the heavy cardboard flaps, I stared, exasperated, at the pieces inside: "Some assembly required."

I hated putting things together—that had been Ray's job. But Abby was due "home" from college in a few days, and I wanted to have a tree up and decorated when she arrived. It would be the only thing that resembled Christmas for her. Abby had celebrated all but one other Christmas in the Colorado house-in-the-woods she had come home to as a sixteen-month-old baby from India.

Her memories included grandmothers, six siblings, and then their spouses and children, and time-tested traditions. This year, it would be just the two of us in the house by the sea she had never called home and had only briefly visited. So we needed that tree, decorated with familiar ornaments, to anchor both her and me in this unsettled time.

Gazing into that box, I assessed the possibilities of how to integrate yet another of Ray's responsibilities. I chose option two from the list I had previously compiled: learn something new, then do it. Although it took all evening to match the black-and-white pictures on the written directions with the colors and textures within that box, I did it.

The ornaments were a different kind of hard. Ray and I had exchanged Christmas ornaments throughout our marriage. Every year we bought each other one we thought best represented our year or portrayed a special memory. Sometimes our decisions were mutual—like the years our grandchildren arrived. Other times they differed. Each ornament came with a memory and a story.

Decorating our Christmas tree had become a walk down memory lane. There were children, grandchildren, and new puppy ornaments. Airplane and suitcase ornaments represented vacations and international ministry travel. Bride and groom ornaments celebrated the year two daughters and one son got married within five months of each other. The ambulance reminded us of the seizure Abby suffered during her first Christmas in our family. Memories of graduations, Hope's Promise, and the heartfelt speech Ray delivered at a company meeting had all dangled from golden threads in front of twinkling lights.

That year I unpacked the ornaments of "what was" during a holiday season, that plunged me into "what will come" . . . in our family, in our traditions, in me without Ray.

Abby caught the red-eye from Portland and arrived in the

early hours of a mid-December morning. She was exhausted, her body depleted. She had scrambled to save the first semester of her junior year after missing three weeks of classes when Ray died. I took her to urgent care, where she was diagnosed with two ear infections and pneumonia on top of her asthma. Then she slept, for a very long time.

We limped into Christmas cobbling together a handful of traditions with others we tweaked, like Indian food for our Christmas Eve dinner instead of the annual crab bread.

Abby and I enjoyed our time together and filled our days with beach walks and long talks, road trips, and local excursions. But Christmas had been an in-between time—a placeholder until we found our footing as a family. Its passing brought relief and gratitude that we had survived our first holiday season without Ray.

Fear and dread shrank in the wake of these milestones. Still, I protected margin in my life to accommodate the unfinished rhythm of grief. I placed few demands on my time or energy and gave myself space. I attended church but sat on the aisle in case I needed to leave. I scheduled commitments sparingly. Healing required me to stay with the messiness of loss for as long as it took.

Nearly four months after Ray's death, with administrative tasks waning and holiday milestones behind me, I dared to lift a corner of the present to peek into a future without him. I looked not only at the day-at-a-time existence I had been living, but also at what a string of days linked together for the rest of my life could look like. I felt trapped by how long and hard that future, measured not in hours or days—but in weeks, months, and years—might be. Like sucking air in hard labor before the birth of a child, it was an I'm-so-done-with-this-and-want-to-go-home-now kind of hard.

A body that betrayed, untamed time, and emotional space had spawned unsettledness. Then it rattled around where roles, responsibilities, and significance had reigned.

I had found worth in my roles as wife, mother, and social worker / executive, but when they were replaced almost simultaneously by widowhood, empty nest, and retirement, my sense of purpose collapsed. In Ray's absence I had looked to family members and friends for my sense of affirmation. But I knew it was not their job to make me feel good about myself or my decisions. Meaning for my repurposed life had to come from within.

I sensed God bidding me to wait amid the echoes in these empty places, to resist "doing," to be still, to allow him to realign my thoughts with his love and acceptance, and to gently reshape me from who I was into the woman he had created me to become.

The needs of others had driven my schedule for more than four decades. Managing family life and a professional career had created chaotic, yet dependable, rhythms and purpose.

With roles now gone, I awoke to white space on my calendar that offered opportunity yet tempted apathy. I remembered God's invitation: *Follow me. I want to recover your life.* Following had led to unsettledness. Like a mending wound that itches and begs to be scratched, unsettledness had become an uncomfortable part of my healing process.

I made peace with waiting for God to stoop and pick up the shattered pieces he would use to recover my life from loss and rearrange them into a mosaic that would tell my story of redemption. I also listened for what pieces I needed to let go of.

Quiet Reflections

- Describe a time when you felt out of sync with yourself or were unsettled. Where did you see God in the messiness, and what did you learn through that experience?

- When have you seen life unfold in healthy, life-giving ways? What helps you notice these times of unfolding?

- Describe what it feels like to wait. What would it look like for you to wait on God to recover your life?

Chapter 15

Letting Go

*When we truly pray a goodbye
we enter into the whole matter; we live it.
We connect our life with God and
bring our pain into that intimate relationship and
know that the touch of God is the touch of healing.*
—Joyce Rupp, *Praying Our Goodbyes*

October 2015–December 2016

Creation sobs outside my window. Swollen, low-hanging clouds shed their tears in torrential outbursts for days, punctuated by hiccups and drizzle in historic proportions. Sheets of rain pummel my home as water with no place to go transforms my patio and flat backyard into a wading pool. Besieged blades of grass peek above the water's surface as if straining to survive. Cooper and Annie refuse to go out. "You're kidding, right, Mom?" they seem to ask as Hurricane Joaquin threatens landfall.

A product of complex weather patterns, this category-four hurricane devasted parts of the Bahamas in October 2015 and claimed the lives of thirty-three crew members on a cargo ship at sea. Although it never made landfall on the continental United States, Joaquin ransacked parts of the Eastern Seaboard with drenching rains and coastal flooding.

My first hurricane watch lent a reflective backdrop to grief; creation mirrored this slice of my life. Record-breaking moisture, complex emotional patterns, and low-hanging clouds that didn't budge.

In the aftermath of company, I accepted this forced hibernation as easily as my next breath. Within solitude's cocoon, I considered this question: Lord, why am I here? The answer took root and grew from within: my time in North Carolina would be about letting go and praying my goodbyes. Teetering on the cusp of uncharted territory, I suspected this shakeup to extend beyond grieving Ray and the future we would never share—that it would stretch wider and run deeper. It did, leaving no area of my life untouched.

Praying our Goodbyes: A Spiritual Companion through Life's Losses and Sorrows by Joyce Rupp mentored me throughout this nineteen-month sojourn as the Lord used circumstances, his Word, and the Holy Spirit to gently reveal the extent of this purge and the transforming power of letting go. Rupp explains, "The reality of moving on is this: We can never do so until we let go of whatever binds us to the past."[18] I had wound together the dangling threads of my unfinished business and spun a web that bound me to the past. Letting go would stretch me.

Rupp offers four aspects to praying our goodbyes that helped me understand the process: recognition, reflection, ritualization, and reorientation. These emotional and spiritual markers, progressive points on an internal recovery map, shepherded me toward a predetermined path: *Follow me. I want to recover your life.*

My journey has not been straightforward or efficient. I crashed through warning signs, careened into detours, got stuck in the weeds, drank too much wine, and indulged myself with magnificent pity parties along the way. Sometimes I hid in one place for a long time. I circled others, afraid to come in for the landing. Some letting go happened in pieces, over time, as I returned to tackle the same issue, doing what I could each time. The language of this paradigm offered a plan and a way to monitor my progress. It also provided the grace of a traveling companion and kept me from getting lost.

Recognition required me to identify and name my loss and the pain I experienced because of it. Praying my goodbyes to Ray took time. Grief tethered me to him, and I didn't want to let that connection go; it was all I had left.

Recognizing the losses his death created was what I imagine waking up in the ER with multiple injuries caused by one accident might be like. It took months to assess the damage and courage to look beneath each bandage and describe what I saw and felt. Not all loss was the same. The pervasive grief his absence inflicted was different from the episodic pain of grief triggers or doing something new without him.

Reflection invited me "to become comfortable with slowing down, with stillness, with solitude and aloneness, with not being afraid to look inward or to go deeper."[19] It allowed time to choose the perspective from which I would tell my story: gracious or bitter, healing or wounded, hopeful or resigned to simply waking up each morning. Reflection offered a long-term view of our short-term stay on earth and cultivated gratitude for God's watchful, faithful care over my life. It compelled clarity about sin, regret, guilt, and the unfathomable grace of forgiveness.

Ritualization applies imagery or symbol, and movements in prayer when "we connect our hurt with the God of healing. It is the whole of our person which is at prayer."[20] I didn't expect praying my goodbyes to Ray would be a one-and-done deal. But nearly nine months after his death, I ritualized my intent to release the pain of his loss with candles, photographs, and prayers of thanksgiving and letting go. It helped me continue to give God permission to tinker in the painful, tender places of my heart to recover my life.

Reorientation happens when we bring faith into our healing and find the courage to go on. My social work education had taught me that it takes five to seven years to adjust to a major life transition. I had sustained significant ones: death of a spouse, cross-country move, empty nest, and retirement. More lurked. Reorientation would take time, patience, and grace.

Letting go became worship, another rhythm of grace in this season of loss.

My mother died in February 2016, five months after Ray. Mom relocated from her home in Kansas into an apartment in Colorado two years before Ray and I moved to North Carolina. She wanted to live nearby yet retain her independence. I took her to doctor appointments and out to lunch, and I did her grocery shopping. Mom joined us for dinners and family celebrations. The two of us made regular trips to the library, and she loved to go shopping for new shoes. Ray and I picked her up on summer Saturday mornings to go to the farmers' market with us and out for coffee. He ran errands for her and helped around her apartment. I treasured this time with her. I had not lived in the same town with Mom since I left home after high school to work in Colorado and then on to college in Arkansas.

She suffered her first heart attack when she was forty-eight and survived two more, as well as a stroke and several major surgeries, by the time she moved. We helped put her affairs in order, knowing she could die at any time. It was understood, however, that I would care for her until then.

Once we decided to move, Ray and I dreaded the looming conversation.

"Mom, we have some hard things to talk about," I said apologetically, steering our conversation toward what we needed to say the afternoon we went to tell her. She stiffened in her chair and clenched her jaw, bracing for bad news—a response both sad and familiar to me. "Ray and I have decided to move to North Carolina," I began. "He can breathe better at sea level and wants a quality of life, for whatever time he has left, that he can't have at this altitude."

I paused to collect myself and let Mom do the same as we struggled to hold back tears. "I hope you know this isn't a decision we've made lightly," I added. "We have considered the ramifications our leaving will have." As tears replaced words, Ray watched helplessly from across the room.

She said she understood. Her best friend also suffered from interstitial lung disease and was on the national waiting list for a lung transplant at the time. Then we cursed this wretched disease and how deeply it affected us all.

Ray and I met with our children and their spouses a few days later to discuss our move. We shared a list of ways we had been helping Mom and the name and contact information of her service providers. They agreed to divvy up the responsibilities between themselves, glad to be able to help.

They loved their grandma and cared well for her in our absence. But they weren't me. Mom had relinquished her life to care for her mother when she could no longer live alone. I was expected to do the same.

Once Ray died, she assumed I would immediately return to Colorado. "But Mom, I don't have a home to return to," I lamented, having finalized the sale of our home three days after Ray died. "I haven't even unpacked from this move. I can't up and leave. I'm too exhausted to move back now."

She disagreed. Although I texted daily and called her frequently throughout the fall of 2015, we seldom spoke of me returning to Colorado. But our difference of opinion remained the elephant in the room—at least for me.

Mom was admitted to the hospital in January 2016 following a stroke-like neurological incident. After her discharge and for the next six weeks, my siblings and I rotated staying with her. Jeff drove in from Oklahoma to relieve Kristi. A week later I flew from North Carolina to replace Jeff, then Kristi returned from Virginia. This cycle repeated itself until five days before Mom died, when the three of us and Jeff's wife, Linn, kept vigil. Hospice nurses and grandchildren flowed in and out. Friends called or stopped to say goodbye.

A new grandson was born days before Mom died, raising the emotional stakes for me. Ray would never hold and pray for this grandchild as he had done with eight others. And facing Mom's death without his support, while grieving his death, compounded my losses. Tears of sorrow and joy plunged into the same bucket, the one with Ray's name on it.

I wrestled with unmet expectations in the weeks after Mom died: those I held for myself and ones my mother had of me. I had failed and disappointed her. I reflected on other decisions Ray and I had made throughout his illness. Some, like agreeing to all the prescribed pharmaceutical interventions, I would redo. But not our cross-country move or my decision to stay in North Carolina—I would make them again. Every. Single. Time.

That "aha" gently loosened the edges of stuck places enough to let in the light, and I let go of unmet expectations. Had Ray and I not moved, Jeff, Kristi, and I would have missed the opportunity to share in Mom's care, strengthen our relationship, and all be with her when she died. Had I returned to Colorado immediately after Ray's death, I would have forfeited the most spiritually rich time in my life, which had been decades in the making.

I'm sorry my mother felt abandoned when Ray and I moved . . . so very, very sorry. I probably would have felt the same way. Although I tried to do right by both Ray and Mom, I had to choose.

I hope she has forgiven me.

Five months after Mom died, I had a hip replacement. The orthopedic surgeon opined that a genetic predisposition and lifestyle issues were probably to blame—and yes, he said, grief undoubtedly exacerbated and accelerated my hip's expiration date.

According to the Harvard Health Publishing website, "The grief of losing a spouse or partner affects not just emotional and mental health, but physical health as well. Numerous studies show that the surviving spouse or partner is likely to develop health problems in the weeks and months that follow."[21]

I was an overachiever. The same surgeon replaced my second hip in December, five months after the first one. Underscoring these emotional and physical losses, my immune system crashed, paving the way for recurring bouts of bronchitis, pneumonia, and a smorgasbord of infections.

I discovered a host of healing graces nestled within these losses as I journaled through tears and pain. I owned my part in our decision to move and let go of guilt about my mother. I had done the best I could. I let Mom's response be hers.

Humbled by physical limitations, I began to shed my self-sufficiency and gratefully received an outpouring of support from family and friends. Instead of harboring expectations to reclaim my former self, I hunted for the gift in circumstances that continued to sideline me. Amid these losses and contrary to what appeared otherwise, a still small voice insisted: *Follow me. I want to recover your life.*

It was in the letting go that reached beyond death to plumb the foundations of faith and expose lies I believed. Lies that whispered:

You can't survive Ray's death.

Your worth depends on achievement.

You need to wear yourself out for God and be all used up.

You can do it all and have it all.

You can improve yourself until you are acceptable to yourself and others.

Letting go of lies and exchanging them for truth slowly transformed my perspective of God. When measured in days, this was imperceptible, but it was significant when seen over weeks and months. Learning to receive what he has done for me birthed peace and comfort. Sorrow offered surrender and deepening trust in the gentleness and kindness of Jesus. Those gifts would have remained unopened if my years of trying to outrun sorrow had prevailed.

Letting go of the values and rhythms from my former life of striving, achieving, hurrying, and producing allowed me to claim new ones that fit a season of healing and restoration: grace, peace, gratitude, contentment, and joy.

Letting go of "shoulds" created margin in my life. As I opened wide my heart to the presence of God, his unforced rhythms of grace began to rearrange the landscape of my heart, sculpting it to hold the experience of his presence. When I let go of busyness, strength in stillness found me. Solitude became my friend. As I let go of marriage, a lifestyle I loved, I opened the gift of personal freedom.

Praying my goodbyes allowed me to honor aspects of my life that suited me for a season. Once honored, I could let go of what no longer fit, didn't work, or had already been taken away. Letting go was a plumb line I held close to remind me of the purpose of my unscripted season. In the nineteen-month interlude before I would return home to Colorado, I wanted to finish well. Letting go chipped away at pretenses to reveal authentic places in my heart; it became a spiritual practice that drew me closer to God.

Letting go, however, was not a linear, one-and-done affair. Issues resurfaced. Old habits sneaked back in stressful, unguarded times. But as I followed and slowly released what bound me to my past, I experienced the presence of God in new and life-giving ways. His presence defeated my crisis of faith by showing me his answer: He was enough for today. He reset my internal compass and had begun, in bits and pieces of time, to satisfy the deepest longings of my heart in ways I didn't expect. And then, this . . .

Quiet Reflections

- Identify one of the things in your life that has bound you to the past (wounds, lies, values, rhythms or schedules, culture, family, etc.)? Take a few minutes to name it and bring it before God. What do you want him to do for you?

- Consider your losses. Take time to name these losses and the pain you have experienced because of them. Prayerfully visualize sharing your list with Jesus and linger there. What do you notice?

- What decision in your life would you like to redo? How have you dealt with the reality of that decision and its consequences? If that decision has not been reconciled, what is the next right step to take? If it has been reconciled, how did that happen?

Chapter 16

Beloved

*We were not created to possess ideas about God but
to be possessed by him in the way a husband and
wife possess each other through loving commitment
and intimate attraction. God fashioned us for love,
and all heaven holds its breath to see
if we will love him back.*
—Judith Hougen, *Transformed into Fire*

Come away, my beloved.
Song of Songs 8:14

July 2016

It's the middle of nesting season now. Loggerheads come
ashore to lay their eggs in response to primordial knowing
that has guided them since a breath after time began.

Crawling from the ocean onto her natal beach in the dark of
night, a female loggerhead begins to search for a place to lay her
eggs. Slow and awkward on land, she carves a wavy wake in the
sand, leaving unmistakable tracks as she heaves herself beyond the

high tide line into the fringe of first vegetation, perhaps beside the rise of a dune or log.

With her front flippers, she makes a trial sweep. If it meets her approval, she begins to excavate her nest. She scrapes away sand, then sculpts a body pit in which to settle herself. Once level with the surrounding beach, her back flippers dig deep to form a flask-shaped, slightly lopsided, spherical egg chamber, creating space for new life to incubate and grow. Exhausted, she rests.

When her strength returns, the loggerhead fills her nest with leathery pliable eggs the size of Ping-Pong balls. Two to three at a time, she drops them into the darkness until she's laid, on average, 120 of them. Then, guided by the song of the ocean and the moon's reflection on lapping waves, she returns the way she came—back into the sea.[22]

Named for the characteristic strong, broad head, loggerheads begin life by clambering from their underground nests as mere two-inch, two-ounce hatchlings. If the turtles survive the predators awaiting their harrowing dash to the ocean and other hunters therein, they can grow to an average of three feet in length and top 375 pounds. Loggerheads are the most abundant marine turtle species in US coastal waters, with southeastern beaches among the two largest nesting areas in the world.

These solitary creatures remain invisible during much of their time at sea, migrating vast distances between feeding grounds and their breeding and nesting sites, where only females come ashore to nest.

But not just on any shore. Each female returns to the beach where she hatched to lay her own eggs. Although scientists can't explain with certainty how she does it, this intrinsic sense of knowing has guided her home since God created ocean creatures, blessed them, and said, "Be fruitful and increase in number and fill the water in the seas" (Gen. 1:22).

I enjoy taking family and friends to the Karen Beasley Sea Turtle Rescue and Rehabilitation Center when they come to visit. The local attraction is staffed by volunteers and championed by the community where I live. The nature center not only operates a hospital to rescue, rehabilitate, and release wounded sea turtles back into the ocean; it also provides educational tours to the public and trains college interns. Through their Turtle Project Nesting Program, they survey the twenty-six miles of Topsail Island's coastline each day from May through August to identify and protect sea turtle nests.

Knowing that only one in one thousand hatchlings will survive their first year of life, employees and volunteers help ensure safe passage to the sea at night for newly hatched turtles. The dedication of those who care for these creatures has inspired me, as have the turtles themselves. How could something so silent and ancient possibly touch me so deeply?

Another Saturday night ebbed and flowed, the texture of time loose and flat like the edges of tide scattered upon the shore. Typical rhythms skewed. A murky puddle of minutes and hours drifted within smudgy borders of sunrise and sunset.

Dark then, inside and out, all was quiet. I closed the shades and turned on a lamp. Curling into a corner of the couch, I settled within its glow. Annie and Cooper sprawled beneath my feet, sleeping. Soft muzzles quivered, relaxed, then surrendered to doggie snores. I reached for the novel I'd been reading about a young woman named Mattie, married to a fisherman and living on one of Florida's countless islands.[23]

So far, we had little in common, Mattie and me. Until that night, when halfway through the book her husband perished at sea. I wept with this now-kindred spirit, her pain my own. And watched as page after page she struggled to redeem her loss and pull together pieces of her husband's life to keep his memory alive.

I stopped. It was time. After more than forty years, the knowing in my soul said it was time.

Returning the book to the coffee table in front of me, I rose, walked across the living room and down the hall into my office, and switched on the light. Standing in front of the closet, I opened its doors. I stretched, slid the box from the upper shelf, lowered it to the floor beside my chair, and sat down. Then I reached into the box to gently remove a letter, yellowed and warped by time. Slipping the folded page from the envelope, I exhaled—a slow, jagged breath I didn't know I'd been holding—and began to read.

Ray and I wrote almost daily letters to each other during a yearlong, long-distance dating relationship and engagement. We both saved them. I stored them together in one box after we married and shoved it to the back of various closet shelves as we moved from home to home through more than four decades of marriage. I knew I would someday read them again.

I did on that Saturday night. Absorbed within its garbled time, I read and cried—one letter after another. Welcoming the return of lost memories, I read of friends with whom we had shared our faith journey, our deepening romance, and the meaningful places that held our story. The words swept away time, creating a place for me to settle.

Love and longing flowed through the decades into the wee hours of Sunday morning. I couldn't stop crying tears of loss, remembrance, and gratitude.

I finally slept a few hours, attended church, then returned to my chair to read more letters that chronicled our desire to be together, our decision to marry, and the pain of frequent goodbyes.

As I finished reading 322 letters shortly before noon on Monday, I felt something had changed, physical and spiritual. What had begun as a stirring in my heart had swelled into a seismic shift from upside down to right side up. Words digging deep, creating space for life to incubate and grow, had gently sculpted my soul for what it was created to hold.

Words of longing also awakened grief, making a holy mess of sorrow. It was suffocating. Longing for Ray crushed my heart. Claustrophobic, I felt trapped within overwhelming sadness and dread of this long goodbye. At the same time, I felt the healing power of words shaping a nest in me to nurture new life.

The words spoke into my pain, piercing the place in my heart where such things are stored—and they've come tumbling out. I was trying to grieve judgment free and unashamed, with grace for myself as I trust my Father to lead me to safe harbor. But it was messy. Very messy.

Ray didn't journal or keep a diary. After he died, I hungered and searched for words, things he'd maybe written on scraps of paper: directions, a phone message, bank balance, or grocery list. I hoped they would satisfy a hunger I couldn't name.

Until that Saturday night. A year's worth of letters—filled with love, longing, dreams, humor, questions, and everyday events. Words in his handwriting. Words that outlived him. Words that began to heal my broken heart.

My heart heard Ray read his letters to me. Not as a mature sixty-five-year-old man, but as a passionate young man growing into adulthood, fearful he wouldn't be a good enough husband or father, desperately wanting the approval of his father and mine—a young man with unwavering faith and wild love for his bride-to-be.

When Ray died and his hugs, soft eyes, and words went away, I asked God to help me believe he would be enough—enough on messy days and at night when I'm undone by Ray's empty side of our bed. I asked God to be enough as I grow old alone. I wanted more than to know *about* God's love. I wanted to experience the awe, the belonging, and foreverness of it. I wanted to feel satisfied, full, and fulfilled. I wanted to be whole.

At the core of my longing clung this question: Will I ever feel loved again? Then amid the puddle of minutes and hours drifting within borders of sunrise and sunset over three days, Ray's words began to fill the space that silence, solitude, surrender, and letting go had created. But there was more.

Beneath the echoes of Ray's words, I felt another voice: one that held his words and breathed life into them until they found their home in my heart. I knew God had used Ray's words to infuse my heart with God's love for me: *I am his beloved.*

This was not the only time I had felt or experienced God's love for me. But this time it held a deeper meaning, a reassurance that God was with me and loved me in this season. It was the beginning of how I would learn to receive my Maker as my husband (Isaiah 54:5).

The same knowing that guides a turtle home to her natal beach had brought me to this beach to excavate my soul's terrain and carve unmistakable tracks on my journey of coming home to myself, to sweep and scrape away, to dig deeper, to create space in my soul for the presence of God.

I am his beloved. Overcome by its fullness, I bury my face in my hands and sob. My only response to this love that turned my heart right side up and filled it to overflowing is to love him back.

Quiet Reflections

- What ideas do you have about God that prevent you from being possessed by him in the way a husband and wife possess each other through their "loving commitment and intimate attraction" to each other? What is the source of that resistance? What unsettles you now?

- Describe a time when something in nature, God's word, or a piece of art touched you deeply. With what longing in your heart did it connect? How did you respond?

- Knowing about God's love and experiencing that you are his beloved are vastly different from each other yet integral to a meaningful relationship with Jesus. When and how have you experienced God's love for you? What was your response? If you haven't, take a moment to share the desire of your heart with God.

A New Kind of Broken

*People with regrets can be redeemed, but they cannot
reverse the loss that gave rise to regrets . . .
They must somehow transcend what lies behind
and reach forward to what lies ahead . . .
They must seek personal transformation,
which comes only through grace.*
—Jerry Sittser, *A Grace Disguised*

*If we confess our sins, he is faithful and just
and will forgive us our sins and
purify us from all unrighteousness.*
1 John 1:9

August 2016

Reading our letters awakened the past and inspired a humbling, exhausting stretch of my letting-go journey. Recent hip replacement surgery sidelined me, affording the time it would take. Christmas Evans, a Welsh preacher in the late eighteenth and early nineteenth centuries, reached through time to show me the way.

One Sunday afternoon I was traveling by horseback to an appointment. Suddenly as I went along a very lonely road, I was convicted of having a cold heart. I dismounted, tethered my horse to a tree, and found a secluded spot. Then, walking back and forth in agony, *I reviewed my life* [emphasis added]. I waited before God in brokenness and sorrow for three hours. Finally, a sweet sense of His forgiving love broke over me and I received a fresh filling of His Holy Spirit. As the sun was setting, I walked back to the road, found my horse, and rode on to my appointment.

The following day I preached with so much new power, to a vast gathering of people on a hillside, that revival broke out and ultimately spread through all of Wales.[24]

Although Evans's situation did not describe mine, he did validate whispers niggling around the edges of my spirit: *We need to go back before we can go forward.* Evans's story gave me the courage to look back without fear of getting stuck in the past—seeing it as preparation for living into my future—a step toward recovering my life.

Maybe now *was* the time to read over forty years' worth of journals and diaries—*my* life review. I liked the young woman who wrote those letters. I wanted to understand the wife and mother she had become and glean what counsel she offered as I sought answers to these questions: What are my continuing questions and lifelong interests? What themes mark my life? Why am I who I am? How will these insights impact my future? I offered these questions as prayer and plumb line when I pulled the first journal from a dusty box, settled into my chair, and began to read.

I started in the seventies and plowed through the eighties. Early married and young family years rendered memories sacred and tender when seen through the lens of time.

But I got stuck in the nineties. I grew deeply disappointed as I saw myself in the context of my family during that stressful decade: two demanding careers, teenagers testing boundaries at one end of the parenting spectrum, and young adopted daughters struggling and teetering on the other. Reading my journals exhausted me. I revisited hectic schedules, conflict, and prayers that begged God to wave a magic wand while I remained unwilling to make the tough decisions required to curtail a reckless, relentless striving to do it all.

It took weeks to read through those hard years. It was painful. Shame wrestled with grace as I read and wept my way through the nineties. With the wisdom of age, I saw that mine was not an intentional derailing or rebellion, but a misguided sense of serving God and family that flowed from untended wounds and an inflated sense of responsibility. Remorse ushered me into a new kind of brokenness: repentance.

I was guilty of Alan Fadling's observation in *An Unhurried Life*. "Many of us measure our faithfulness to God by how many tasks we get done for him or how many meetings we attend to plan his kingdom work. As glad as he is for our service, I believe he is even more pleased when we give him our attention and our friendship."[25]

Having experienced the grace of knowing I am God's beloved allowed me to sit with him in brokenness, sorrow, and regret. As I watched the driven me being swept farther from God's heart and my own, I felt compassion for the wounded young woman I had been, striving for acceptance and approval.

"Loss takes what we might do and turns it into what we can never do," laments Jerry Sittser in *A Grace Disguised*. "It forces us to recognize the incompleteness of life and to admit our failures. Regret is therefore an unavoidable result of any loss, for in loss we lose the tomorrow that we needed to make right our yesterday or today."[26] Regret forced me to admit the pain I had caused others and to let go of a tomorrow I would never have to apologize to Ray. Yet I could still make peace with regret.

"If we confess our sins, he is faithful and just and will forgive us our sins and purify us from all unrighteousness" (1John 1:9).

Forgiveness is not Jesus *and* community service or good works. I had trusted in Christ for my salvation yet labored to prove I was worth the investment. I could never do enough.

So I let him be enough. Then sobbed grateful tears for his forgiveness and the grace to forgive myself. And in those tears, I discovered that God was graciously recovering my life through repentance.

"The closest communion with God, I have begun to discover, comes through the shedding of my tears," notes Fil Anderson in his book *Running on Empty.*[27] He continues, "I've been living in the growing awareness that God wants me to admit my brokenness and let my Inventor heal my severely damaged self-image."[28]

God has graciously done the same for me in the gentlest, kindest ways. He replaced certain lies with his truth and relieved me of some of the baggage I had accumulated through the years. What remains he is growing into an uncluttered and more authentic, yet unfinished woman.

Repentance—an owning, seeking forgiveness, and letting go of sin and regret—cleared the way for coming home to me. This erupted into gratitude as the first anniversary of Ray's death approached and brought healing answers for how to commemorate it.

September 2016

I didn't exactly dread the day. I did acknowledge that it ticked off another milestone, though the day itself would be no different from the preceding 364 others. I didn't need a date on the calendar to remind me Ray was gone. But still, how would I spend the day? I considered how the parallel tracks of unpredictable and intentional had coursed through my journey over the past year.

Grief triggers, for example, were unpredictable. They were out there, but I didn't know when they would strike or how I would respond. It could be a funeral procession or walking through the men's section in a department store. Overhead oldies music in the grocery store made my knees buckle. A car that looked like his or bald men in striped polo shirts evoked a second, longing look. Routine rhythms of life had sabotaged me: visiting grandchildren alone, emptying the dishwasher, walking the dogs, or catching a glimpse of his likeness in one of our children was dangerous territory. I navigated a landscape filled with landmines each day and braced myself against the emotional capital they consumed, like the last swirls of water being sucked down a drain.

But I'd also made intentional choices, like praying with my sons at the foot of Ray's deathbed and deciding to take care of myself. I used an unlimited book budget to learn from others. I ritualized my letting gos and created new traditions—like giving myself gifts from Ray on Christmas, my birthday, and Valentine's Day. That would make him smile, and it has given me something to look forward to.

I chose to focus on gratitude that first anniversary—perhaps as defense against the unpredictable, but primarily because I wanted to establish a trajectory for the years and milestones to come and ease my children's sorrow and awkwardness about this and future anniversaries.

I was grateful for many things: my home, church, and neighborhood friends; family and friends who visited me in North Carolina; the freshness of the presence of God; and the beach. I was thankful Ray and I had moved to North Carolina and for two new grandchildren. I reflected on events leading up to Ray's death—the roles our children had played in supporting our move, taking Ray fishing, coming to the hospital for last goodbyes, helping me unpack, doing work around the house, and planning his service—and their phone calls, pictures, texts, gifts, and visits in the months that followed.

I wrote and mailed a letter to each of my children and their families to thank them for their specific acts of kindness, generosity, and sacrifice, and concluded all seven letters with this:

I want to mark this first anniversary of your dad's passing with gratitude. I'm thankful I was married to my best friend for over 42 years; that God blessed us with incredible children, sons and daughters-in-law, and grandchildren; that Ray brought me to North Carolina and the Lord will take me home to Colorado. I'm thankful for this set-apart time and that I've begun to appreciate the gifts of solitude, silence, sorrow, surrender, and the sweet side of suffering. I'm thankful for my Savior, for heaven, and that a grand reunion awaits Ray and me once this long goodbye is over. And I'm thankful for the support I've received on this unscripted journey.

But I also want to mark this first anniversary with a renewed hope and vision for the future—a future that will unfold without Dad's physical presence but one that will build on the legacy he wanted to leave. I hope we will take the memories and traditions that nourish our souls and help us become better people, parents, and family members. And that we will forgive and let go of those that do not. Our rich family history and shared sorrow provide fertile ground for the seeds of grace and compassion to grow strong and deep. May we:

Love one another unashamedly
Forgive one another freely
Pray for one another fervently
Spend time with one another often
Expect the best of one another unwaveringly
Speak kindly to one another always
Share our joys and burdens authentically
Encourage one another consistently
And pass our faith to the next generation diligently.

Thank you for all you have done for me during this past year. You are such a blessing to me. And I look forward to the opportunities we will have to write the next great chapter.

By then, the words of Jesus from Mark 5:19 had begun to rattle around in me: "Go home to your own people and tell them how much the Lord has done for you, and how he has had mercy on you." My time in North Carolina was both sacred and temporary. Only a few months remained before I would return to Colorado and walk into the next chapter of learning to be me without him.

Quiet Reflections

- What are some of your grief triggers? How do you navigate the landmines and brace yourself for the emotional capital they require?

- When have you lived from a misguided sense of serving God and family? What impact has it had on you and others? What advice would you offer to your younger self?

- Healing requires that we go back before we can go forward. With that thought in mind, take a few moments to quiet your heart. Where is God inviting you to go with him?

Song of the Ocean

All through the dream of creation God is singing his
song of ravishing delight for those with ears to hear.
There are ways you can open your soul to that song:
places where it is more easily heard,
practices that attune the ear of your heart,
people who will help you listen.
And in that song you can discover
who you really are.
—Chris Webb, *God Soaked Life*

The Lord is my strength and my song.
Exodus 15:2 ESV

March 2017

Sipping my second cup of coffee, I watched flames dance in
the fireplace, more ambiance than warmth, although outdoor
temperatures were unseasonably cold. Early-morning sun peeking through the window highlighted the blanket of dust on my
coffee table, and I wondered what I would do about it.

My time in North Carolina was ending. I had begun to make choices about how I would leave and say last goodbyes to this place and those I called friends while honoring the rhythms of grace this season had birthed.

I had done well my letting go over the past nineteen months; only one remained. I had wrestled for months to understand a growing conviction that God was asking me to let go of my children. I could not, would not, stop being their mom or loving them. It wasn't about relinquishing our history, the memories we shared, or the new ones we would make. So what was I to let go?

I listened and looked deep into what bound me to the past until I landed here: God was asking me to let go of my agenda for each of my children and to trust him and his plan for their lives. They were grown and on their own, and I needed to let their story be their story and just love them. No more parenting required.

Joyce Rupp, in *Praying Our Goodbyes,* reminded me that "letting go is an *attitude* that grows within us. It is never complete until it is acted upon."[29] My final ritual would come later.

But that morning by the fire, I considered what I would carry with me from my time in North Carolina. I would carry gratitude for ways God gently comforted my heart and opened my eyes to grace all around me. I'd carry healthier perspectives and insights gained from lingering with Jesus. I would carry hope for my future and a plan to return to this place as often as I could. I'd carry kindness and gentleness toward others, particularly those who suffer—and we all suffer. I would carry commitments to listen more than I talk, maintain margin in my life, and remain attentive to God's presence. I would carry freedom and rest in my soul that comes with receiving what Jesus freely gives. I'd carry healing from the song of the ocean. I would carry my internal compass and walk toward "home." And I would carry grace to forgive myself in the countless ways I would fail in each of these.

"One goes into the wilderness to be taught, not to stay," Paula D'Arcy taught me in her book *Gift of the Redbird.* "Then the task is to come out and carry the message to those with whom you live."[30]

It was time for me to go home.

"Mom," said my oldest son, Chad, when he called one day as I prepared to leave, "I've been talking to the others, and we want to help you make the drive back home. We know that's what Dad would want us to do. He took you there, and we'd like to help bring you home."

Gratitude and relief washed over me. I was concerned about making that four-day trip with two big dogs and two hips not fully recovered from their bionic makeover. Chad outlined possible scenarios he and his six siblings had discussed. In the end, Brooke flew out to drive the first three days with me, and Nick escorted me home from Kansas City.

I had known I would return home alone, but leaving wasn't that simple. Colorado might be home, but I felt at home in the south, near the water. I would leave with a heavy heart, wondering how to integrate my need for both places that had found a home in me. The woman returning to Colorado had been made different in the crucible of set-apart time.

Because I wanted to finish well, I had to tend to unfinished business. From the time I understood God was asking me to let go of the agenda I had for my children, I considered ways to ritualize this goodbye. Making the abstract concrete, I began by writing Chad's name at the top of a blank sheet of paper, then listed my agendas for him in bullet points beneath his name. I continued through the birth order of my seven children until I had completed this process for all of them. No judgment, just an honest assessment between me and God. Then I drew a line through each list and prayed my goodbyes, releasing my children from any obligation to live their lives according to my desires for them. I surrendered. *Not my will but yours be done.*

But I wasn't done. I had collected seventeen flat stones on a series of beach walks, one for each of my seven children and ten grandchildren, and wrote one of their names in black ink on each stone. I placed them in a Ziplock bag and tucked it in a kitchen drawer until it was time.

I filled my last days with overseeing movers pack and load my belongings onto a truck, meeting with friends, sharing final meals and goodbyes with neighbors and church friends, and accepting help with packing my car. Then I drove to the beach one last time.

I pulled into a parking space overlooking the deserted coastline on a chilly March morning and absorbed the beauty of the seascape sprawling before me. This ocean both held and reshaped my story. I traced the changes in me back to this.

The ocean helped me heal. Not only from the personal grief of Ray's death and an unrivaled season of loss, but through a universal kinship with suffering that nurtured compassion. The Jesus I'd come to know in these sorrows is gentle and kind. His yoke is easy and his burden light, because when I let him, he has carried my load. He is powerful and mysterious, making whole, tender, and healthy that which was broken. Hope and healing, receiving and restoration, sorrow and surrender had shifted the narrative of my story.

My solitary time had been about unlearning, relearning, and learning. Love and inside-out transformation had sustained me. I had found grace waiting when I quit trying to outrun suffering and accepted comfort in my sorrows. I'd seen God's faithfulness when I prayed: "Teach me your way, Lord" (Ps. 86:11). I'd shed rhythms that no longer fit the shape of my repurposed life and received new ones suited for this season. I had learned to rest, linger, and listen to his voice.

And one of the places I hear God best is near the ocean.

"The voice of the LORD is over the waters" (Ps. 29:3). His song grounds me in the ebb and flow of generations passing through time, and my place in his story. Created on the third day, "the Spirit of God was hovering over the waters" (Gen. 1:2b). That same spirit had been hovering when grief took root in me as I watched Hans bobbing alone in turquoise water in Bora Bora and the evening seventeen years later when Ray and I picnicked here on the threshold of his death. The ocean sang of eternity and had turned my heart toward home.

"The LORD your God is in your midst, a mighty one who will save; he will rejoice over you with gladness; he will quiet you by his love; he will exult over you with loud singing" (Zeph. 3:17 ESV). Each time I had come to this beach—to think and pray, to be quiet and still—I had heard his song.

The song of the ocean is a metaphor for healing that has begun in me. Physical sights and sounds of waves breaking on the beach mirror waves of grace that have broken through barriers to reach my soul. It is the song God sang over me as he held me until acceptance, gratitude, perspective, and a heart made new by his love found me. It got messy and was seldom pretty, and I'm sure it's not over. But the ocean opened my soul to God's song because in it I saw his reflection.

The ocean is relentless. I'm rendered speechless each time I crest the dune, hear the roar, and see waves racing up the beach to greet me. Its majesty calms me and gently reaches to accept another fragment of grief when I'm ready to let it go.

The ocean is powerful. I am not. Not as fault or defect, but by design as a vessel in the hands of the potter. Awed by this holy awareness of my minuscule, transient place, I experience the peace of surrender. He has counted the grains of sand my toes nuzzle and attends to every detail of my life. His heart toward me, his beloved, amid this beauty evokes tears of worship.

The ocean proclaims mystery—not to be mastered, understood, quantified, or reduced to systematic theology, but to be received as a gift to remind me whose I am. It humiliates my attempts to humanize God. Mystery validates my longing to dwell in its presence. It opens my eyes to see grace in dying and hears amid grief an invitation to recover my life. It requires me to listen with eyes and heart wide open.

As I prepared to leave North Carolina, I was humbled by this: God had orchestrated this time and place, just as he summoned the birds at the cemetery and the feather on the beach. In myriad other ways, he has shown himself faithful. He reoriented the position (right side up) and posture (open, receiving) of my heart to hold the experience of his presence. He did this so I would know that yes, indeed, he is enough.

By God's grace, I have survived that which I feared I could not.

I picked up the bag of named stones from the seat beside me in the car, then strolled to the water's edge. Barefoot, I stood in that intersected space of sand and water as waves ebbed and flowed onto the beach. Following a wave into retreat, I spilled the stones onto the sand, then bent to turn them name-side up. Standing, I watched the next wave wrap itself around my offering and draw the small pile of stones back into the ocean—accepting what I was letting go and entrusting to God's care. No longer wife or parenting mother, I released what bound me to the past. If God is enough for me, he will be enough for them when they ask.

I turned to leave. Sea breeze swept through my hair, and my bare feet savored this last delicious walk in the sand. I climbed into my car, looked back at the spot on the beach where my altar had been, and drove away, over the bridge to the mainland, past my old neighborhood, and turned left onto Highway 17 toward Wilmington, where I would meet Brooke's plane.

Tomorrow we would begin my journey home.

Quiet Reflections

- Where are the places in your life where you most easily hear God's voice? What makes them special? What do you notice about God and about you when you are there?

- Who are the people in your life who have helped you along your spiritual journey? How did they do that? For whom might you be such a person?

- "The Lord your God is in your midst, a mighty one who will save; he will rejoice over you with gladness; he will quiet you by his love; he will exult over you with loud singing" (Zeph. 3:17 ESV). And then you said . . .

Part Four

Safe Harbor

And while the journey to this place of rest
and receptivity can be hard,
and we can find ourselves stripped down
and painstakingly remade along the way,
we arrive grateful. After all, we are finally
where we belong: close to the Father's heart.
Our long and challenging road has,
in the end, brought us home.
—Chris Webb, *God Soaked Life*

Keeping It between the Ditches

Even to your old age and gray hairs
I am he, I am he who will sustain you.
I have made you and I will carry you;
I will sustain you and I will rescue you. . . .
I say, "My purpose will stand, and
I will do all that I please." . . .
What I have said, that I will bring about;
what I have planned, that I will do.
Isaiah 46:4, 10–11

March–June 2017, Colorado

I'm going home, but I'm not. Things have changed. New buildings cling to once-vacant lots, traffic has burgeoned, and life here has continued fast forward while I paused. Free of rhythms and responsibilities that once tethered me to this place, I remain vigilant about what to add: life-giving relationships, adventures, and purpose. And what to forgo: busyness, "shoulds," and assumptions regarding just about everything. In this new season, I want to remain open, expectant, and brave. To say yes to what is not unethical, illegal, or unbiblical as I try new things and discover pieces of my repurposed life.

Four days after leaving North Carolina, I pulled into the driveway of my "starting over" home. I had flown back six weeks earlier to find a house, then closed on it via FedEx in time for my end-of-the-month arrival. Unpacking and settling in took weeks. By June I felt ready to schedule the first of two appointments I planned to make after I got back.

When life slung me into the pit of depression several years ago, I discovered my brokenness and God's grace in the muck. Carol, a gifted counselor, led me out. I suspected grief might test my emotional health. So nearly two years after Ray's death, I wanted her perspective on how I was doing.

"What are your goals for counseling?" she asked after we greeted each other, exchanged pleasantries, and settled into our chairs.

"I need you to help me keep it between the ditches," I said. The temptation to minimize and move on flanked one side of my journey, while depression beckoned from the other.

She chuckled, jotted a note on her tablet, and waited for me to continue.

"All I have is my experience and history, and nothing to compare it to. I want to grieve well so I can move forward well but not slip back into depression or get stuck."

Nodding, she clasped her hands and leaned toward me. "Okay," she murmured. "Let's pray." We bowed in this familiar ritual of previous times together as we silently invited the Lord to direct our time, to quiet our minds and hearts. And to surrender.

My tears began after we prayed. Carol paused, waiting. "Tell me what that's about," she gently coaxed.

"I'm just sad," I whispered.

"But what's behind the sad?"

I didn't know. There was no in-front or behind sad, only encompassing sad—like being helplessly suspended in a vat of Jell-O sad.

Sensing my confusion, Carol handed me a copy of the feeling wheel, a tool that maps feelings and looks like bicycle spokes with names of emotions radiating from a hub of primary feelings. Neat and tidy. Concrete words. Perfectly spaced straight lines separated one feeling from another. Each spoke linked nuanced feelings with major ones, like artists organizing color hues on a wheel, a visual relationship between primary, secondary, and tertiary colors. Connected. Related. Yet each holding its unique expression and meaning.

Leaning forward from the overstuffed chair beside her desk in the warmly lit, bookshelf-lined office, I took the diagram and settled back to examine it. I found "sad" in the center and read the name of each emotion behind it—emotions that were often expressions of sadness. There were twelve, as diverse as depressed, sleepy, bashful, and inferior. I read them again, willing the right word to find me.

"None of these words really describes it," I finally said, handing the paper back to her. "But the closest is depressed."

She nodded knowingly before we continued.

I thought about that counseling session over the next few days, recalling my tears and the feeling wheel. I'm sure Carol and I talked more about depression, but I don't remember. It was a second word on that feeling wheel—guilt, that kept niggling me for more attention.

I dismissed it at the time, kicked it to the curb, and tried to make it disappear the split second it caught my eye. I had made peace with regret when confronted with it during my life review. Now guilt laid siege to my pondering. Uncensored thoughts erupted and tangled themselves into a hideous web of accusation: I was responsible for Ray's death. It was the only way God could get my attention; had I surrendered sooner, the kids might still have their dad and the grandkids their Bum. I could have made him happier. I didn't deserve to grow, let go, move on, or be happy.

I felt guilty, but I wasn't—except to acknowledge, for these brief moments, the guilt whose voice I sought to silence. Allowing it to speak exposed the lies and highlighted my choices: wallow here or exchange them for God's truth. Keeping it between the ditches required me to choose the latter.

I am no more responsible for Ray's death than I am for the rising and setting of the sun. God numbered Ray's days before he was born. His death was part of the life cycle in our fallen world, as is my sadness and longing to be with him. Of course, I could have made him happier. We both would have liked a few do-overs in our marriage.

That God would bathe this season in grace is pure gift, made richer by one gift that has taken the longest to see—the gift that brings me to my knees. Confused and afraid, I had pleaded with God in the hours before Ray died, questioning his sufficiency to sustain me in this loss and satisfy me in the future. These words had given me hope: "Teach me your way, Lord, that I may rely on your faithfulness" (Ps. 86:11). They became a lifeline as I prayed through unfamiliar terrain in the days, weeks, and months to follow. And offered insight during my life review.

When Ray asked that long-ago Saturday morning, "Where do you want to go for your retirement vacation?" I answered without a second thought. For reasons I don't understand and can't explain, I have been drawn to North Carolina since I was a young girl.

The gift of grace that took the longest to see is this: God began to orchestrate his answer to my crisis of faith prayer decades before I cried out to him from behind the wheel of my car in a hospital parking lot. He wove together my childhood infatuation with horses, a pony named Misty who lived on an island, my love of all things beach and water, a trip to Bora Bora, a move to coastal North Carolina for a set-apart season with him, and two gold wedding bands engraved with the beginning and ending of our story to show me his faithfulness.

Ray and I chose Bible verses before we married to convey our commitment to each other and had the references engraved in our wedding bands. I chose Ruth 1:16–17 (NASB) for Ray: "But Ruth said, 'Do not plead with me to leave you or to turn back from following you; for where you go, I will go, and where you sleep, I will sleep. Your people shall be my people, and your God, my God. Where you die, I will die, and there I will be buried. May the LORD do to me, and worse, if anything but death separates me from you.'"

Several months after Ray died, I read the book of Ruth, awed by the prophetic overtones and newfound hope. Elimelek, along with his wife, Naomi, and their two sons, left Bethlehem because of a famine to live in neighboring Moab, a territory often in conflict with the Israelites. Elimelek died there, leaving Naomi widowed with two sons, who married Moabite women. After they had been there about ten years, both sons died. Later, when Naomi heard there was food in her homeland, she made plans to return there with her two daughters-in-law. One turned back. But Ruth loved Naomi and chose to leave her own people and go with her. As the story progressed through four short chapters, Ruth met Boaz, a relative of Elimelek, and they married. In time a son, Obed, was born. He was a blessing to Naomi in her old age and became the father of Jesse, who was the father of David in a lineage that culminated in the birth of Christ.

God had cradled their story within his own.

I identified with Ruth and Naomi's circumstances as widows:

each had been taken to a land of strangers and there encountered God's faithfulness as he recovered their lives from loss. I was living in the echoes of their story, waiting for God's unfolding of my story.

Ray selected Ephesians 5:25–27 (NASB) for me, which reads in part: "Husbands, love your wives, just as Christ also loved the church and gave Himself up for her, so that He might sanctify her, having cleansed her by the washing of water with the word, that He might present to Himself the church in all her glory."

Ray felt compelled to get to North Carolina. The place where he got the girl back that he had married. The place I followed him to. The place where Ray would die and God would answer my deepest prayer in a deeply personal way.

"I'm sorry," Ray had whispered as he lay dying.

"About what?" I asked, dumbfounded, as I caressed his hand and searched his eyes.

"It wasn't supposed to turn out this way," he said.

Ray had promised to love me as Christ loved the church. He didn't do it perfectly. He could be manipulative and sarcastic. We endured unholy hours, days, and seasons in our marriage, but we always found our way back. Ephesians 5:25–27 was a commitment he took seriously and shared with our children, one he encouraged our sons to make to their wives when they married.

I believe Ray was driven to get to North Carolina because that was where he presented me to the Father eighteen hundred miles from home in a land of strangers, devoid of that which made my life my life, so I could experience the undistracted fulfillment of answered prayer. God's presence and the redeeming transformation of my heart were God's resounding answer: "Yes. I am enough."

In pondering the power of prayer, unhindered by time, Ken Gire opines that prayer has the power of "reaching across time to take the broken pieces of a person's life and gently place them into what can only be described as a divine work."[31]

Did Ray follow God's leading? Did God use Ray's desire to breathe better at sea level to move us to North Carolina? Or did our story just happen? I don't know; it's part of the mystery. But I do know this: Ray's commitment to love me as Christ loved the church didn't die with him; his death completed it.

This amputation of oneness with its seared, jagged edges left dangling and throbbing—and my aloneness—carved a doorway through which I limped into a deeper relationship between Jesus and myself. Jerry Sittser, in *A Grace Disguised,* wrote: "Redemption is rooted in a paradox, which can be summed up in a simple phrase: we become who we already are in Jesus Christ."[32]

I have changed.

I like the changes. So would Ray. Oh, how I long to tell the love of my life this redeeming story. Sorrow and repentance flowed freely. Words became few. Peace replaced anxiety, at least for some of the time. Rest found me. Silence and solitude befriended me. Margin invited me to linger and enjoy God's presence. Scripture comforted my heart. The ocean nourished my soul. Surrender felt safe and strong and right. Ray and I set out on our last big adventure together, and it became the ride of a lifetime.

God *is* recovering my life from loss, and I am coming home to me.

For now, Carol says, I'm keeping it between the ditches.

Quiet Reflections

- When you look back over the course of your life, where do you see evidence that God has sustained you, carried you, or rescued you? How have you seen his purposes unfold in your life and family?

- Who helps you "keep it between the ditches?" What are your ditches?

- If you have lost a spouse or loved one, what story would you tell them?

Chapter 20

Tending the Fire

*Our first and foremost task is faithfully to care for
the inward fire so that when it is really needed it
can offer warmth and light to lost travelers.*
—Henri Nouwen, *The Way of the Heart*

March 28, 2018

*I*t took time to find a referral. But one year later I made the
second of two phone calls I planned to make when I got
home. I scheduled an appointment with a spiritual director—after I scoured the website of the retreat house where she worked
for information and pictures.

Scrolling through the roster of staff photos, I found hers.
A friendly face smiled from my computer screen. Not too old
yet comfortably seasoned. Married with grown children, her bio
said. I liked that. This somehow made her more approachable.
And kids—certainly she had experienced both joy and sorrow
with grown ones. That felt significant to me. I liked her stylish,
cropped gray hair, while the alive, joy-filled twinkle in her eye felt

inviting. All this lent credibility to my pursuit: to continue my formational journey.

Author Judith Hougen says that for many Christians, "a terrible chasm yawns between knowing and experiencing, fact and faith, ideas and action. In short, there's a disconnection between the head and the heart."[33] That was true for me, since my childhood response to God had been all but erased as I grew into adulthood.

Although I wasn't raised in a churchgoing family, we did attend sporadically during my early grade-school years. I never understood why we sometimes did but most of the time didn't go to church. Our rhythm seemed like the silent transition of one season changing into another: we went for a while, and then we didn't until we went for a while again. Until finally the rhythm, like that of a dying heart, stopped.

My earliest memories of church and God are of sitting in the back of the sanctuary between my parents. Hushed murmurings as others arrived and greeted one another in whispers or with a nod. And seeing my white anklets at the end of short legs that didn't reach the ground when we bowed to pray.

What I remember most, however, is the beauty of the sanctuary: deep maroon carpet and mauve pew cushions; sunlight glimmering through stained-glass windows molded into pictures of Mary and baby Jesus and grown-up Jesus carrying a lamb; and the enormity of the large wooden cross that dominated the rear of the altar. Simple. Elegant. Unavoidable.

Chills shivered through my body when majestic organ chords thundered, signaling the choir to begin their soulful stroll down the aisle and for the rest of us to rise and sing along. I felt grown up. Holding my own hymnal, I tried to match the words I sang with the up and down movement of the musical score in front of me as two by two the choir members entered the sanctuary from behind us. Different heads atop matching white robes glided down the aisle and up the stage steps until they filled the choir lofts, and the song came to an end.

Then wordless rustling as we all sat down.

I felt comfort and peace. The calm, still reverence was unrivaled by any other experience in my world. I felt small but not insignificant. Certain hymns, like "Holy, Holy, Holy," attached themselves to my little-girl heart and moved it in ways I now recognize as worship. I felt a certain "at homeness" there—something in me I didn't know how to name responded to Something in this place that was apart and separate from and did not include my parents.

Before I had an ounce of spiritual understanding, religious training, or language to describe my experience, my soul declared itself: I responded to God with my heart.

Before the external rhythms of going to church finally died, seeds of longing and desire had been sown. They remained dormant for years yet were intuitively nurtured by the rhythms of a heart searching for home.

When given the opportunity to trust Christ as my Savior on a Young Life ski trip to Colorado during my junior year in high school, I said "Yes!" But two years later, when I got involved with a campus ministry, my emotional response to God got sidelined for years, creating my own chasm and disconnection between head and heart.

"Together the heart and head constitute the self whom we are and the self who engages life on all levels," Hougen says. "We're created to establish belief through two pathways—cognitive and experiential, that is, head and heart. And only when both pathways are engaged does belief become complete and actual." Like her, "I required not more information but deep response, not to feed the head but to ignite the heart."[34]

I had experienced that integration of head and heart during my time in North Carolina. I intended to continue with my spiritual formation journey—"a process," says Robert Mulholland, "of being conformed to the image of Christ for the sake of others." It is "the great reversal: from acting to bring about the desired results in our lives to being acted upon by God and responding in ways that allow God to bring about God's purposes."[35]

A key element of that process can be a spiritual director, a person trained in spiritual practices who helps others discern the subtle ways God is making himself known and encourages those with whom they work to respond to his leading in their lives. Spiritual direction helps cultivate intimacy with God.

When I said yes to the invitation to *Follow me . . . I want to recover your life,* this was where Jesus took me—closer to my Father's heart and subsequently closer to my own. I could not go back.

My internet research done, the appointment made, I grabbed my jacket and rushed out the door for my first appointment with a spiritual director. Mentally calculating the quickest route, I drove through home turf, over the railroad tracks, through Sedalia, and out Highway 67. Nearing the retreat grounds, I recalled my previous visits.

My first was several years earlier when I came for a half-day Hope's Promise leadership retreat. A morning of solitude with a list of suggested Bible verses to prayerfully consider as we sought direction for the future of our orphan care ministry. Curious about this mysterious place near my home, I was pleased when a staff member suggested we meet there. It had felt off limits to me: I wasn't Catholic. I pictured secret rooms where monks and out-of-touch clerics hovered over ancient scrolls in burlap robes. Intimidated by its "Catholic-ness" and the grandness of the manse nestled on spacious grounds, I assumed I didn't belong. Creating further distance was the required silence during our retreat—a challenge for an extrovert. Maybe a half-day retreat had been a good place to start.

I returned over the years for day-long personal retreats—to pray for guidance as the executive director of Hope's Promise and for my personal life. I found comfort in the silence of the small room on the second floor where I read, prayed, and sought God's counsel, and in walking the beautiful grounds that embraced the rugged beauty of this Colorado valley. My memories were rich and good. I looked forward to my return that day, wondering what role this place might play in my life.

I turned from the two-lane highway onto a winding asphalt lane that meandered up a hill to the retreat house, a massive, two-story structure spilling over the hillside. I was returning as a changed woman, inside and out, a pilgrim reshaped by sorrow and pain and God's healing graces. How would that affect this experience?

Tension swelled as I wheeled into the parking lot. Not knowing what to expect and with fear that my spiritual language was inadequate for this experience, I wrestled with the sense that I was right where I belonged. I was learning to accommodate such tension; it reminded me I was forging ahead into an unscripted future.

Dreariness hovered as I climbed from the car: grays and browns painted the sky and earth while shed leaves from barren trees bunched and decayed in haphazard piles against stands of naked scrub oak. I walked across the graveled parking lot, my crunching steps a solitary sound. This trek to the front door, across a driveway, and up a serpentine sidewalk felt longer than I remembered. I slowed to relish the joy and gratitude that swelled in me.

Opening the heavy wooden door, I stepped into familiar comfort. Deep green carpet, a cozy fire crackling from across the room, and love seats and chairs inviting sojourners to stop and rest. Silence filled this place, creating space to wait for the One who is the same yesterday, today, and tomorrow.

I peeked into the small, pleasant office with her name above the door. Like the rest of the retreat house, it was open and inviting. A modest desk and jacket-strewn chair filled one corner. Bold paintings depicting biblical themes of relationship and connection adorned the walls in frames intended for a bigger space. I liked it. The office fit the woman's picture on the website. When she appeared moments later, smiling as she strode from the hallway into her office, she invited me to sit.

"Would you like some water or tea?" she added.

"Water please," I said then followed her to the dining room, where we filled our glasses from a large receptacle. Back in her office, we sat facing each other. Swishing gray bangs from her forehead, she bought moments to collect her thoughts and, I assumed, to decide where to begin with me—a habit, a reminder perhaps, to pray for guidance and wisdom.

"Tell me what brings you here for spiritual direction," she began. A big, wide, open-ended question, one I would ask a client on their first visit to my office. She didn't take notes like a counselor but listened as a friend.

Efficiently sorting through memories and culling key ones to most accurately portray my story, I began: gnawing spiritual hunger, the adoption of three daughters, depression, a terminal disease, a cross-country move, Ray's death, Mom's death, two hip replacements, letting go, new rhythms, moving home, deciding which pieces of my life to keep and which to replace—and following Jesus into a further journey that today had led me to her door.

Tears surprised me in the telling of my story to one who would gently hold such things. She commented with teaching and insight and then paused before asking another question. I presumed she was assessing my comments and discerning where to go next as she once again absently brushed aside her errant bangs—an endearing gesture that seemed to allow time for private thoughts as we continued through our allotted time.

"I'm going to give you a passage of Scripture to read," she said a short time later, drawing our time to a close. "It will probably be familiar if you're used to reading Scriptures. But I want you to read it and picture the scene: Who's in it? What do you see? What do you smell? And then ask, Who do you identify with in the scene? What is God saying? And to whom is he saying it? Finally ask, what does it mean to me? Journal what went on in the scene, and tomorrow, read the same Scripture. Ask God to deepen it for you or take you somewhere else."

She rose and stepped to her desk. Turning, she handed me a pink sticky note on which she had written the reference to the assigned passage.

"Feel free to meet with other directors here," she continued, motioning to include those within the scope of the retreat house. "I won't be offended." I received this as an invitation to discuss the next steps.

"Well, I'd like to continue with you unless you sense a check in your spirit about working with me," I said.

No, she smiled and nodded. There were none.

Standing, we hugged. "I like it that you're going to be part of this new season with me," I said, then left the warmth of her office cocoon. Retracing my steps, I opened the doors and stepped into the chilly March afternoon. Pulling my jacket close, I inhaled the damp, earthy smells that greeted me. Life felt right and good as I strolled to my car. I had come full circle.

The yawning chasm between knowing and experiencing had shrunk. Head and heart had become friends and were engaged in a single pursuit. I had responded deeply to the Spirit's invitation in me to Come away, my beloved.

Leaving the retreat house that day, I savored the still and resting landscape and imagined the beauty coming seasons would bring to this place and to me.

That moment, like so many others through which I'd journeyed, had been years in the making. But for now, I was tending the fire . . . and still coming home to me.

Quiet Reflections

- Henri Nouwen says, "Our first and foremost task is faithfully to care for the inward fire." Do you agree with this? Why or why not? How might your tending the fire within you enhance your relationship with God? With others?

- How have you experienced the relationship between your head and your heart? How has that affected your relationship with God? What would you like to change?

- Take a few moments to still yourself. Listen for God's invitation to you. How will you respond?

Epilogue

And the God of all grace, who called you to his eternal glory in Christ, after you have suffered a little while, will himself restore you and make you strong, firm and steadfast.
1 Peter 5:10

Lord, through all the generations you have been our home!
Psalms 90:1 TLB

Christmas Eve 2019

The girls and I scurried to finish up dinner preparations after returning home from our Christmas Eve church service. My heart warmed to see daughters and daughters-in-law as comfortable and at home in my kitchen as I was. We chatted, laughed, sipped wine, and divvied out tasks until platters of our traditional crab bread meal and candlelight adorned the dining room table, extended by four leaves and spilling into the hallway. We circled up to pray, then squeezed into more chairs around the table than it was made to accommodate.

Our fifth Christmas without Ray.

Nick sat in Ray's place at the head of the table. Three-year-old Joel clambered into the chair beside me at the other end, his towhead and big hazel eyes barely visible above the tabletop. As good-natured banter tumbled from happy hearts and we passed the food among us, Joel scrambled to his knees. Straining over those next to him to get Nick's attention, he blurted, "Hey! Uncle Nick! Do you know how to cross your eyes?"

Not missing a beat, Nick showed Joel in comical ways, accompanied by a hilarious monologue that, yes, he knew how to cross his eyes. Everyone roared. Chuckling, I laid down my fork and savored the moment: laughter, noise, trust, and the comfort of my family.

Look at this, God whispered. *This is what I have done and what I continue to do for you.*

When I had returned home nearly three years ago, I wondered how I would adjust to the busyness and drama of real life and what my "just Mom" role would look like. I lived alone in the suburbs. My children had families and lives of their own, as did I.

"Mom, how do you see the leadership of our family happening now that Dad is gone?" Tyler asked one afternoon when he and I met in his office shortly after I arrived home.

"Well, I am the matriarch," I teased, yet grateful for his question that acknowledged the shift in family dynamics and the questions it raised for us. "But I don't want to be boss of the world," I continued. "I love the group process. Everybody's voice counts and needs to be heard."

We continued to discuss how we would work together when problems arose. We agreed that gathering as an extended family was a priority, especially with young cousins living in three states. My goal was unity amid our diversity. I silently prayed for a spirit of grace and forgiveness to permeate our family, though it has not always been so. There are many differences among us: race (Indian, Asian, Black, and Caucasian), faith, politics, personalities, and economics, to name a few of the potential landmines.

Basking in the warmth around my table, I watched Christmas Eve dinner arrange itself into a crowning culmination of numerous dress rehearsals since my return. I had survived the grief of Ray's death, and as a family we were learning to do life without him.

"We get together so frequently that we are all very comfortable with one another," Nick had recently commented. "We know there aren't going to be any unexpected surprises."

We found our rhythms in daily life and celebrating milestones—like Joel's birth and the adoption of his younger cousin Lydia Rae; grandson Corbin's high school graduation and starting college; a family reunion in Breckenridge; and recurring holiday and birthday celebrations.

Other milestones, however, demanded something more.

Ray's death had created two significant losses for Abby, our youngest daughter, who was twenty when he died. She grieved that her daddy would not see her graduate from college or walk her down the aisle when she married. The rest of us did the best we could to help make both events meaningful for her.

I drove to Oregon one month after I drove from North Carolina to Colorado; Abby's siblings arrived by plane and car. We convened outside Portland to celebrate her graduation from George Fox University, pack four years' worth of her belongings, and move her home. Within two days she accepted a full-time position in her chosen profession as a social worker.

Almost two years later, Abby married Camden, her high school sweetheart, in the historic, country chapel near Ray's grave. She gave me the honor of walking her down the aisle. When asked "Who gives this woman?" her six siblings and I rose to say, "We do."

Abby had pictured getting married in the winter with bridesmaids dressed in red since she was a little girl. Their intimate

February wedding, complete with snow-covered grounds and the white chapel with a bright-red door, fulfilled that dream. She and Camden thoughtfully crafted the details of their wedding ceremony and reception to reflect their values of faith, family, friendship, and second chances, as well as their personalities and relationship.

Abby looked stunning in a black-and-gold traditional Indian salwar kameez. Her study abroad in India as a college junior and a bad experience with a traditional bridal shop paved the way for her to include pieces of her birth culture in her wedding. She had grown into a young woman at peace with the tensions inherent in her story and her dual heritage.

After the ceremony, guests mingled outside the rural chapel nestled within a grove of pine trees at the base of the foothills. Before joining the reception, Abby and Camden made their way down the snow-covered lane to Ray's grave. As the sun slid behind the hills, splashing its farewell in pink and orange across a crisp, winter sky, she stooped to caress the outline of his name etched in granite and pressed her hand against the cross engraved between his name and mine on the joint headstone. Then Abby knelt to share a private moment with her dad before leaving her bouquet behind. Ray was remembered and honored, but the celebrations were for Abby and Camden. Their ceremony had marked an ending and a new beginning. They were now a military family with the United States Air Force. Shortly thereafter they moved to Louisiana, where Camden had been stationed.

There have been other, more subtle changes. Although fishing trips with Ray have ended, our sons continued the tradition with an upgrade. They now take their sons *and* their daughters on annual fishing, camping, or backpacking trips and get together to fish as brothers when schedules allow.

God continues to recover my life, a one-of-a-kind mosaic he is creating from remnants of the past—longtime friends, community, and church family—with new friendships and adventures. I've integrated protecting white space on my calendar with a social life.

Recovering my life has been rooted in a deepening relationship with God. I trust him. I love him. I am grateful for his forgiveness, salvation, and everyday blessings. Receiving what he has done for me has fostered compassion for others. I no longer waste time in self-flagellation and try to treat myself and others with the gentleness and kindness I've received from him. I am content and like my repurposed life.

I resumed speaking at foster and adoptive mom retreats and led adoptive mom support groups for a time. I share life with like-minded friends through writing, hiking, and spiritual formation groups, and with family members who live nearby. I visit out-of-state children and grandchildren and take road trips when I get the urge. Cooper, Annie, and I have settled nicely into our negotiated relationship: they snuggle and listen, and I give them free room and board.

I celebrate annual "Sib Reunions" with my sister, brother, and his wife—a tradition birthed in the wake of our father's death. We gather each July and fill our days with travel, laughter, food, hiking, and a train ride if we can find one. We stay up past our bedtimes to tell and retell stories that still make us laugh, cry, or rage at injustices we've suffered. And I return to the beach as often as I can.

That fifth-anniversary Christmas Eve, as laughter waned and eating resumed around my table, a simple epiphany, hidden in plain sight, found me: we're going to make it.

I drove to the cemetery and parked the car. Snug in my wool winter coat, I walked to Ray's grave, now marked by a headstone with both our names. Seashells from Topsail Island nestle within Colorado river rock that borders this memorial—a testament to both places that found a home in our hearts. The perfect fishing lure and a piece of bubble gum left by one son, and a golf ball commemorating the annual Hope's Promise golf tournament, now held in Ray's honor, silently shout our need to remember, honor, and include him even as we go on without him.

Shortly before he died, I asked Ray one last time, "Are you afraid?"

"No," he said. "Not for me. Just for you and the kids."

I had come to tell him, "You don't need to be afraid for us anymore." Ray was with us that Christmas Eve. He had settled in us . . . the memories, the stories, the ways he loved us and wounded us, and the space in our hearts he now occupies. We are learning to hold the indelible prints he made in our lives and allow them to grow, mature, and manifest themselves in the changing fabric of our family.

My eyes and heart tasted answered prayer as we sat around the table, lingering there long after dinner. Ray and I had splurged to buy that table years ago because we envisioned its sturdy, oval shape surrounded by laughing children—and one day by their spouses and children. This table that holds our imperfect story could tell of birthday dinners, heated debates, conflicted silence, a wedding reception buffet, blackberry cobbler on Christmas Eve, countless card games, and years of nightly family dinners.

My lover, best friend, and teammate is gone, but I'm still in the race. Although I'm certain there will be new trials ahead, I hope to continue the legacy we began and finish well for both of us.

Out of the crucible of grief, I have come home to the comfort of people and places that share our story, to the essence of the person God has created me to be, and to experience the gracious presence of God, my soul's true home.

Acknowledgments

Above all else, I am grateful to my heavenly Father, who, in the crucible of grief, answered my deepest prayer by showing me that yes, he would be enough to help me survive what I feared I could not. That he would continue to bless me through the love and generosity of his people in the living and telling of this story is pure grace. I am humbled and deeply grateful. This story would not have been the same without them.

My deepest thanks to Ruth Bowser, who told me she would walk this journey with me and has been true to her word. She holds pieces of my story as only a trusted friend of forty years can do. And Rosie Duggins, longtime friend and writing buddy who, after reading a chapter would sigh, pause, then tell me: "This is the kind of story I would want to read."

Writing group friends, hiking group "belles," and like-minded sojourners in our Sensible Shoes group offered friendship, belonging, and laughter during the writing of this book. Hugs and thanks to all.

Beta readers Paul Lessard, who walked with Ray and me as our pastor through Ray's illness, our move to North Carolina, and Ray's funeral in Colorado; and Pastor Phil Vaughan, who shepherded the church I belonged to during the writing of this book; along with Lori Apon, Tricia Lott Williford, Pat Runyon, Tami Brown, Ruth Bowser, and Kitty Block, who offered encouragement and critique from their respective perspectives as pastors, widows, friends, and writers. Thank you all. Your candid feedback improved this story.

Editors Inger Logelin and Pamela Heim were, for a season, also teachers and mentors. Thank you for your gracious gifts of time, expertise, and lots of red ink. And Maureen Rank, editor and friend, not only helped organize the content and map out timelines but understood the story I wanted to tell, helped me wrestle it down, and encouraged me to hurry up and get it out there. Thank you.

The team at Redemption Press has been delightful to work with. Special thanks to Dori Harrel, Managing Editor, who has gone above and beyond to birth this baby. And Sara Cormany, Project Manager, whose calm spirit and easy laughter were second only to her expertise and professionalism.

Carol Selander has helped me, from time to time, keep it between the ditches. Thank you for how you've influenced my life and for allowing God to use your gifts and your training to serve the body of Christ as a professional counselor.

Friends and neighbors in North Carolina, thank you for welcoming me into your fold and for being vessels of God's grace during my healing season. I treasure the time I had with you and how those memories continue to nourish my soul.

Family and friends who visited me in North Carolina. You came, you listened, you laughed and cried with me, you sat or walked on the beach with me, or cared for me as I recovered from my bionic surgeries. All of you blessed me simply by your presence in those early months.

My sister, Kristi Hellmuth, who from the moment I said "I need you to come now" has been a great friend and the finest of traveling companions on this journey. Thank you.

I offer my deepest love and thanks to my children: Chad (Melissa), Brooke (Erik, deceased), Nick (Jenn), Tyler (Holly), Hope, Sarah, and Abigail (Camden), who have walked segments of this journey with me as they sustained their own loss when their dad died. They have loved and honored me as we continue to learn how to do life together and, in so doing, have honored Ray. He would be so proud.

And to my grandchildren: Corbin, Landon, Jada, Paige, Emery, Eva, Kelly, Lauren, Joel, and Lydia. Thank you for the privilege of being your Mimi and for giving me a greater reason to tell this story. May it point you to Jesus as you grasp your place in the unfolding of God's great story. For *you* are his beloved.

About the Author

Paula Freeman, MSW, is founder and former executive director of Hope's Promise, a Colorado adoption agency and orphan care ministry licensed in Colorado, and author of *A Place I Didn't Belong: Hope for Adoptive Moms.* Widowed with seven grown children, she lives in the Kansas City area but still calls Colorado home—and she gets to the beach as often as she can. Visit her at www.paulasfreeman.com or contact her at paulasfreeman@gmail.com

For more about Hope's Promise adoption and
orphan care and how you can help,
visit them at www.hopespromise.com.

Endnotes

Preface

1 Marilyn Murray Wilson, "Widow Facts," *Creators Syndicate.* August 18, 2017. *www.creators.com/read/positive-aging/08/17/widow-facts* (March 11, 2022).
2 Wilson, "Widow Facts."

Chapter 2: Road Trip

3 Paula Freeman, *A Place I Didn't Belong: Hope for Adoptive Moms* (Franklin, TN: Carpenter's Son Publishing, 2013), 60.
4 Parker J. Palmer, *Let Your Life Speak: Listening for the Voice of Vocation* (San Francisco: John Wiley & Sons, 2002), 56, 61.

Chapter 5: Passing Through

5 David James Duncan, *My Story as Told by Water: Confession, Druidic Rants, Reflections, Bird-Watchings, Fish-Stalkings, Visions, Songs and Prayers Refracting Light, from Living Rivers, in the Age of the Industrial Dark* (Berkeley, Calif.: Counterpoint, 2001), 11.

Chapter 8: Crisis of Faith

6 M. Esther Lovejoy, *The Sweet Side of Suffering: Recognizing God's Best When Facing Life's Worst* (Grand Rapids, Mich.: Discovery House, 2013), 13.
7 Dr. Sanjya Gupta, "Sanjay Gupta's Quest for Better Brain Health," *AARP The Magazine* 63, no. 38 (2020), 35.
8 Emilie Griffin, *Small Surrenders: A Lenten Journey* (Brewster, MA: Paraclete Press, 2007), 162.
9 Lovejoy, *The Sweet Side of Suffering*, 63,72.

Chapter 11: Solitude

10 Henri Nouwen, *The Way of the Heart: The Spirituality of the Desert Fathers and Mothers* (New York: Harper Collins, 1981), *26–27.*

Chapter 12: Follow Me

11 Marjorie J. Thompson, *Soul Feast: An Invitation to the Christian Spiritual Life* (Louisville, KY: Westminster John Knox Press, 2014), 33.
12 Thompson, *Soul Feast*, Summary of Listening in Chapter 3, *Communication and Communion with God: Approaches to Prayer*, 33–36.
13 Charles Stanley, *How to Listen to God* (Nashville, TN: Thomas Nelson, 1985), 154–155.

Chapter 13: Rhythms of Grace

14 Alan Fadling, *An Unhurried Life: Following Jesus' Rhythms of Work and Rest* (Downers Grove, IL: InterVarsity Press, 2013), 9.
15 Fadling, *An Unhurried Life,* 10.
16 Griffin, *Small Surrenders*, 123.

Chapter 14: Unsettled
17 *The American Heritage College Dictionary, Third Edition.* Boston: Houghton Mifflin, 1997.

Chapter 15: Letting Go
18 Joyce Rupp, *Praying Our Goodbyes: A Spiritual Companion Through Life's Losses and Sorrows,* 2nd ed. (Notre Dame, IN: Ave Maria Press, 2009), 79.
19 Rupp, *Praying Our Goodbyes,* 65.
20 Rupp, *Praying Our Goodbyes,* 70.
21 Stephanie Watson, "Death of a Spouse or Partner Can Lead to Heart Attack or Stroke," *Harvard Health Publishing.* February 27, 2014. *www.health.harvard.edu/blog/death-spouse-partner-can-lead-heart-attack-stroke-201402277055* (March 11, 2022).

Chapter 16: Beloved
22 Author's research on sea turtles came from these three websites: Karen Beasley Sea Turtle Rescue and Rehabilitation Center: *www.seaturtlehospital.org* (March 11, 2022). National Geographic Kids: *www.kids.nationalgeographic.com/animals/reptiles/loggerhead-sea-turtle/* (March 11, 2022). Sea Turtle Conservancy: *www.conserveturtles.org* (March 11, 2022).
23 Connie May Fowler, *Remembering Blue* (New York: Ballantine Publishing Group, 2000).

Chapter 17: A New Kind of Broken
24 L. B. Cowan, *Streams in the Desert: 365 Daily Devotional Readings,* ed. James Reimann (Grand Rapids, MI: Zondervan, 1997), 302.
25 Fadling, *An Unhurried Life,*10.
26 Jerry Sittser, *A Grace Disguised* (Grand Rapids, MI: Zondervan, 2004), 96.
27 Fil Anderson, *Running on Empty: Contemplative Spirituality for Overachievers* (Colorado Springs: Waterbrook Press, 2004), 161.
28 Anderson, *Running on Empty,* 67.

Chapter 18: Song of the Ocean
29 Rupp, *Praying Our Goodbyes,* 81.
30 Paula D'Arcy, *Gift of the Red Bird: The Story of a Divine Encounter* (New York: Crossroads Publishing, 1996), 129.

Chapter 19: Keeping it Between the Ditches
31 Ken Gire, *The North Face of God: Hope for the Times When God Seems Indifferent* (Wheaton, IL: Tyndale House, 2005), 126.
32 Sittser, *A Grace Disguised,* 233.

Chapter 20: Tending the Fire
33 Judith Hougen, *Transformed into Fire: An Invitation to Life in the True Self* (Grand Rapids, MI: Kregel Publications, 2002), 20.
34 Hougen, *Transformed into Fire,* 23, 25.
35 M. Robert Mulholland Jr., *Invitation to a Journey: A Road Map for Spiritual Formation, 2nd ed.* (Downer's Grove, IL: InterVarsity Press, 2016), 16, 37.